**OPPOSING
VIEWPOINTS®
SERIES**

Single-Parent Families

Other Books of Related Interest:

Opposing Viewpoints Series
Birth Control
Gender Roles
Teenage Sexuality
Working Women

At Issue Series
Divorce and Children
Has Child Behavior Worsened?
Polygamy
Poverty in America

Current Controversies Series
Abortion
Military Families
Same-Sex Marriage
Violence Against Women

"Congress shall make no law . . . abridging the freedom of speech, or of the press."

First Amendment to the US Constitution

The basic foundation of our democracy is the First Amendment guarantee of freedom of expression. The Opposing Viewpoints series is dedicated to the concept of this basic freedom and the idea that it is more important to practice it than to enshrine it.

OPPOSING
VIEWPOINTS®
SERIES

Single-Parent Families

Margaret Haerens, Book Editor

GREENHAVEN PRESS
A part of Gale, Cengage Learning

GALE
CENGAGE Learning·

Farmington Hills, Mich • San Francisco • New York • Waterville, Maine
Meriden, Conn • Mason, Ohio • Chicago

GALE
CENGAGE Learning·

Judy Galens, *Manager, Frontlist Acquisitions*

For more information, contact:
Greenhaven Press
27500 Drake Rd.
Farmington Hills, MI 48331-3535
Or you can visit our Internet site at gale.cengage.com

Articles in Greenhaven Press anthologies are often edited for length to meet page requirements. In addition, original titles of these works are changed to clearly present the main thesis and to explicitly indicate the author's opinion. Every effort is made to ensure that Greenhaven Press accurately reflects the original intent of the authors. Every effort has been made to trace the owners of copyrighted material.

LIBRARY OF CONGRESS CATALOGING-IN-PUBLICATION DATA

Single-parent families / Margaret Haerens, book editor.
  pages cm. -- (Opposing viewpoints)
Includes bibliographical references and index.
ISBN 978-0-7377-7528-0 (hardback) -- ISBN 978-0-7377-7529-7 (paperback)
1. Single-parent families--Juvenile literature. 2. Single parents--Juvenile literature. 3. Families--Juvenile literature. I. Haerens, Margaret, editor.
HQ759.915.S189 2015
306.85'6--dc23
                          2015028069

Printed in Mexico
1 2 3 4 5 6 7 20 19 18 17 16

Contents

Chapter 3: How Should the Government Treat Single-Parent Families?

Chapter 4: What Policies May Help Single-Parent Families?

Why Consider
Opposing Viewpoints?

> *"The only way in which a human being can make some approach to knowing the whole of a subject is by hearing what can be said about it by persons of every variety of opinion and studying all modes in which it can be looked at by every character of mind. No wise man ever acquired his wisdom in any mode but this."*
>
> John Stuart Mill

In our media-intensive culture it is not difficult to find differing opinions. Thousands of newspapers and magazines and dozens of radio and television talk shows resound with differing points of view. The difficulty lies in deciding which opinion to agree with and which "experts" seem the most credible. The more inundated we become with differing opinions and claims, the more essential it is to hone critical reading and thinking skills to evaluate these ideas. Opposing Viewpoints books address this problem directly by presenting stimulating debates that can be used to enhance and teach these skills. The varied opinions contained in each book examine many different aspects of a single issue. While examining these conveniently edited opposing views, readers can develop critical thinking skills such as the ability to compare and contrast authors' credibility, facts, argumentation styles, use of persuasive techniques, and other stylistic tools. In short, the Opposing Viewpoints Series is an ideal way to attain the higher-level thinking and reading skills so essential in a culture of diverse and contradictory opinions.

In addition to providing a tool for critical thinking, Opposing Viewpoints books challenge readers to question their own strongly held opinions and assumptions. Most people form their opinions on the basis of upbringing, peer pressure, and personal, cultural, or professional bias. By reading carefully balanced opposing views, readers must directly confront new ideas as well as the opinions of those with whom they disagree. This is not to argue simplistically that everyone who reads opposing views will—or should—change his or her opinion. Instead, the series enhances readers' understanding of their own views by encouraging confrontation with opposing ideas. Careful examination of others' views can lead to the readers' understanding of the logical inconsistencies in their own opinions, perspective on why they hold an opinion, and the consideration of the possibility that their opinion requires further evaluation.

Evaluating Other Opinions

To ensure that this type of examination occurs, Opposing Viewpoints books present all types of opinions. Prominent spokespeople on different sides of each issue as well as well-known professionals from many disciplines challenge the reader. An additional goal of the series is to provide a forum for other, less known, or even unpopular viewpoints. The opinion of an ordinary person who has had to make the decision to cut off life support from a terminally ill relative, for example, may be just as valuable and provide just as much insight as a medical ethicist's professional opinion. The editors have two additional purposes in including these less known views. One, the editors encourage readers to respect others' opinions—even when not enhanced by professional credibility. It is only by reading or listening to and objectively evaluating others' ideas that one can determine whether they are worthy of consideration. Two, the inclusion of such viewpoints encourages the important critical thinking skill of objectively evaluating an author's credentials and bias. This evaluation will illuminate an author's reasons for taking a particular stance on an issue and will aid in readers' evaluation of the author's ideas.

It is our hope that these books will give readers a deeper understanding of the issues debated and an appreciation of the complexity of even seemingly simple issues when good and honest people disagree. This awareness is particularly important in a democratic society such as ours in which people enter into public debate to determine the common good. Those with whom one disagrees should not be regarded as enemies but rather as people whose views deserve careful examination and may shed light on one's own.

Thomas Jefferson once said that "difference of opinion leads to inquiry, and inquiry to truth." Jefferson, a broadly educated man, argued that "if a nation expects to be ignorant and free . . . it expects what never was and never will be." As individuals and as a nation, it is imperative that we consider the opinions of others and examine them with skill and discernment. The Opposing Viewpoints series is intended to help readers achieve this goal.

David L. Bender and Bruno Leone,
Founders

Introduction

> *"Raising a family is difficult enough. But it's even more difficult for single parents struggling to make ends meet. They don't need more obstacles. They need more opportunities."*
>
> —Bill Richardson,
> *Address to the Democratic
> National Committee, June 2004*

In the last few months of 2012, a series of protests erupted over working conditions and low wages at Walmart stores across the country. The protests quickly spread to fast-food franchises and became a nationwide protest movement known as Fast Food Forward. As the protests grew, they generated a national debate about the important issue of economic inequality in the United States and the ability of American workers, many of them single parents, to raise a family on the federal minimum wage of $7.25 an hour.

On November 23, 2012, thousands of workers from hundreds of Walmart stores across the country held demonstrations to spread public awareness of the popular chain's controversial labor policies: low pay, poor benefits, and its successful opposition to the unionization of its workers. The protests were timed to impact Black Friday sales, one of the most lucrative sales days of any fiscal year. Although Walmart claims that the demonstrations were small and ineffective, they did generate media coverage of the company's low pay and divisive labor practices.

A week later, an early morning protest erupted at a McDonald's franchise in midtown Manhattan, with the restaurant's morning shift and several dozen workers demanding higher wages and the right to unionize. Over the next few weeks, a series of rallies and walkouts took place at a number of fast-food chains across New York City, including Taco Bell, Wendy's, Burger King, KFC, and Dunkin' Donuts.

As the demonstrations gathered steam and began to spread to other major cities across the country, political and labor activists pressed for better working conditions, access to unionization, and more benefits for working people. The centerpiece of these demands, however, was a raise in the federal minimum wage from $7.25 an hour to $15 an hour. Many of the protestors pointed out that even with a full-time job, they were struggling to keep above the poverty level and were forced to turn to federal benefit programs to make ends meet and feed their families.

A full-time minimum wage worker earns $15,080 a year. The 2015 federal poverty level threshold for an individual is $11,700; the poverty threshold for a family of four is $24,250. A 2013 University of California, Berkeley, Center for Labor Research and Education study analyzed the situation in the fast-food industry: Of 2.2 million men and women working for the ten largest fast-food companies, two-thirds were over the age of twenty, and a significant number were single parents raising more than one child. Fifty-two percent of fast-food workers were forced to turn to government programs, such as food stamps or Medicaid, out of necessity. These programs cost US taxpayers more than $7 billion a year. It was clear to many Americans that the workers had a solid basis for their protest—it was not possible to raise a family on such meager wages without significant government help.

President Barack Obama agreed that it was time to raise the federal minimum wage. In his 2013 State of the Union remarks, he proposed raising it to $9.00 an hour. On March 5, 2013, two Democratic lawmakers, Senator Tom Harkin and Representative George Miller, introduced the Fair Minimum Wage Act, which proposed a raise in the federal minimum wage to $10.10. President Obama quickly voiced his support for the bill. Just ten days later, House Republicans voted it down.

Opponents to the Fair Minimum Wage Act pointed to a Congressional Budget Office (CBO) report that estimated that a half million jobs could be eliminated by 2016 if the federal minimum wage was raised to $10.10 an hour. "This report confirms what we've long known: while helping some, mandating higher wages has real costs, including fewer people working," remarked Brendan Buck, the spokesman for House Speaker John Boehner, in a CBS News report. "With unemployment Americans' top concern, our focus should be creating—not destroying—jobs for those who need them most."

In the subsequent months, protests continued in major cities across the country. They spread from fast-food workers to men and women who worked in other low-wage jobs, including retail and service industries.

Several states, tired of waiting for the US Congress to take action on the minimum wage issue, took the matter into their own hands. In January 2014, minimum wage hikes took effect in fourteen states: New York, Vermont, Ohio, Rhode Island, Florida, Connecticut, New Jersey, Montana, Arizona, California, Colorado, Missouri, Oregon, and Washington.

In 2015 even more states took action on the issue. Minimum wage hikes took effect in twenty-one states and Washington, DC. Connecticut became the first state to raise the minimum wage to $10.10 an hour. Hawaii and Maryland were the next states to follow suit.

The American people largely support raising the federal minimum wage. A January 2015 Hart Research Associates poll revealed that 75 percent of Americans support raising the federal minimum wage to $12.50 an hour by 2020. In addition, 63 percent would support an increase to $15 an hour by 2020.

With so many states taking action on the issue of minimum wage and with strong support from the American people, labor leaders and activists urged Congress to act responsibly and mandate a living wage for millions of workers. "Stagnant income is the crisis of our time, and now is the moment for Congress to act boldly to address it, using one of the most potent tools at its disposal," suggests Christine Owens, executive director of the National Employment Law Project (NELP) in an article at the *Raise the Minimum Wage* blog. "The American people are way ahead of lawmakers on this issue; they have seen cities and states aggressively raise pay while continuing to thrive economically, and they want Washington to do the same."

The struggle to raise the federal minimum wage is one of several key economic issues for single-parent families across the country. The authors of the viewpoints in *Opposing Viewpoints: Single-Parent Families* examine the challenges and effects of single parenting in chapters titled "How Do Single-Parent Families Affect Children and Communities?," "What Challenges Do Single-Parent Families Face?," "How Should the Government Treat Single-Parent Families?," and "What Policies May Help Single-Parent Families?"

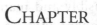

CHAPTER 1

How Do Single-Parent Families Affect Children and Communities?

Chapter Preface

In his 2012 State of the Union address to the nation, US president Barack Obama identified income inequality as the country's central economic and social challenge. He began the speech by recalling the solid middle-class lives led by his maternal grandparents, who were able to work hard, own a home, send their kids to college, and set aside money for retirement. For them, the American dream fulfilled its promise of a middle-class life—a promise that many economic experts believe is becoming more and more difficult to realize in the twenty-first century.

"The defining issue of our time is how to keep that promise alive," President Obama suggested in his address to the nation. "No challenge is more urgent. No debate is more important. We can either settle for a country where a shrinking number of people do really well while a growing number of Americans barely get by, or we can restore an economy where everyone else gets a fair shot, and everyone does their fair share, and everyone plays by the same set of rules."

Income and wealth inequality, specifically the increasing chasm between the rich and poor, has been a growing concern in the United States over the past thirty years. By every statistical measure, the rich are getting richer, the poor are getting poorer, and the middle class is shrinking.

Statistics shed light on the scope of the problem. According to the US Census Bureau, the top 1 percent of the wealthiest people in the country earned 11 percent of all income in 1944. By 2012 that gap had widened to 23 percent. In another troubling marker, the top 20 percent of US households own more than 84 percent of the nation's wealth while the bottom 40 percent own a paltry 0.3 percent. For economic analysts, these numbers demonstrate that the country's wealth is being concentrated among the very wealthy, leaving many Americans scrambling for their share of the American dream.

Other statistics confirm this disappointing trend. While housing prices, utilities, college tuition, and health care costs have soared—the cost of living has increased 67 percent since 1990—incomes for middle-class wage earners have stagnated or fallen. In 2014 the median household income was $51,939 in the United States. If the median household income had kept pace with the economy since 1970, it would now be almost $92,000.

While average American workers have seen their incomes stagnate in relation to the cost of living, corporate executives have seen their incomes skyrocket. Fifty years ago, the average chief executive officer to worker pay ratio was 20 to 1. Today, it has ballooned to 354 to 1, according to an article at the American Federation of Labor and Congress of Industrial Organizations (AFL-CIO) website.

Americans recognize the problem of income inequality and largely endorse President Obama's contention that it is one of the major challenges of our time. According to a June 2015 *New York Times*/CBS News poll, 67 percent of respondents viewed the gap between rich and poor as widening, and 65 percent believe that it needs to be addressed now. A majority of respondents (57 percent) favored government intervention, showing support for such measures as raising taxes on the rich (68 percent), limiting the compensation and benefits of corporate executives (50 percent), and raising the minimum wage from $7.25 per hour to $10.10 per hour (71 percent).

The impact of the rise of single-parent families on the issue of income inequality and economic fairness is one of the subjects explored in the following chapter, which considers the effects of single-parent families on children and communities. Other viewpoints in the chapter examine the changing definition of family in modern society, the benefits of the nuclear family structure to meet the challenges of the twenty-first century, and the effects of family structure and poverty on children.

> "Researchers find that children growing
> up with two married parents are more
> likely to develop 'soft skills' like self-
> control and perseverance that are more
> crucial than ever to school and labor-
> market success."

The Nuclear Family
Is the Best Option for
Children and Society

Kay Hymowitz

*Kay Hymowitz is an author, a journalist, a contributing editor
for* City Journal, *and a fellow at the Manhattan Institute for
Policy Research. In the following viewpoint, she maintains that
children brought up in a nuclear family—father, mother, and
kids—are more likely to achieve economic and family stability
than those raised in other familial arrangements. Hymowitz reviews research showing that nuclear families, which were the
norm in northern Europe and England back to the thirteenth
century, allowed for more flexibility and mobility when it came
to meeting socioeconomic challenges. The nuclear family also
was more child-centered, because mothers tended to be older and
had fewer children, allowing for more focused attention on each*

child. Hymowitz also argues that more mature and experienced parents in nuclear families are able to pass along the kinds of skills necessary to thrive in a demanding, challenging economic and social milieu, thereby giving their children the best chance for success.

As you read, consider the following questions:

1. According to the author, what book presents the most intriguing explanation as to why the nuclear family works so well for kids?

2. What two historians found that the nuclear family was the dominant arrangement in England since the thirteenth century?

3. By what age were most women married in extended families in southern Europe and many parts of Asia and the Middle East around the time of the Industrial Revolution?

Though much of the public seems unaware of it, family scholars believe that—generally speaking—children are best off growing up with their two married parents. These are the children most likely to get the education crucial for maintaining a middle-class life in an advanced economy, to remain stably employed, and to marry and raise their own children to go on and do the same.

A Rational Explanation

But it is not well understood *why* the married couple—or nuclear family—works so well for kids. The most intriguing explanation I've seen can be found in a little-known 2002 book by the sociologist Brigitte Berger: *The Family in the Modern Age.* It recalls an old-fashioned era of sociology. There are no charts, regressions, or metrics; it is, rather, an exposition of economic, social, and demographic history. Yet it manages to anticipate and explain what today's empirically grounded sociologists have repeatedly discovered about families and child well-being.

And so to Berger's history: Not so long ago, family scholars labored under the assumption, half-Marxist [referring to the political, economic, and social theories of Karl Marx], half-"functionalist," that before the Industrial Revolution, the extended family was the norm in the Western world. There was more than a little romanticism associated with this view: Extended families were imagined to have lived in warm, cohesive rural communities where men and women worked together on farms or in small cottage industries. That way of life, went the thinking, ended when industrialization wrenched rural folk away from their cottages and villages into the teeming, anonymous city, sent men into the factories, and consigned women to domestic drudgery. Worse, by upending the household economy, the Industrial Revolution seriously weakened the family. The nuclear family, it was believed, was evidence of family decline.

But by the second half of the twentieth century, one by one these assumptions were overturned. First to go was the alleged prevalence of the extended family. Combing through English parish records and other demographic sources, historians like Peter Laslett and Alan MacFarlane discovered that the nuclear family—a mother, father and child(ren) in a "simple house," as Laslett put it—was the dominant arrangement in England stretching back to the thirteenth century.

Rather than remaining in or marrying into the family home, as was the case in southern Europe and many parts of Asia and the Middle East, young couples in England were expected to establish their own household. That meant that men and women married later than in other parts of the world, only after they had saved enough money to set up an independent home. By the time they were ready to tie the knot, their own parents were often deceased, making multigenerational households a relative rarity.

The Advantages of the Nuclear Family

Far from being weaker than an extended family clan, Berger shows, the ordinary nuclear family was able to adapt superbly to changing economic and political realities. In fact, the family arrangement so common to England helps explain why it and other nations of northwest Europe were the birthplace of the Industrial Revolution, the launching ground for modern affluence. The young nuclear family had to be flexible and mobile as it searched for opportunity and property. Forced to rely on their own ingenuity, its members also needed to plan for the future and develop bourgeois habits of work and saving.

These habits were of little use to the idle, landed rich who were wedded to, and defined by, the ancestral property: think *Downton Abbey* [British drama series]. Similarly, in extended families, a newly married couple was required to move in with the larger maternal or paternal clan and to work the family land or maintain the family trade. Under those circumstances, people, particularly women, married young, generally before 20. Between their youth and dependence, the couple was not capable of becoming effective strivers in a changing economy.

These observations are not unique to *The Family in the Modern Age*. But Berger finds another less appreciated advantage to the nuclear family: It was uniquely child-centered. In societies that rely on extended families, young women had plenty of time to have five or more children. The older brides of northwest Europe, on the other hand, had fewer fertile years ahead of them and smaller families, which enabled them to provide more focused attention on each child. Their children became part of a household already steeped in an ethos of hard work, future-mindedness, and ingenuity. This prepared them to take advantage of the new modes of labor in-

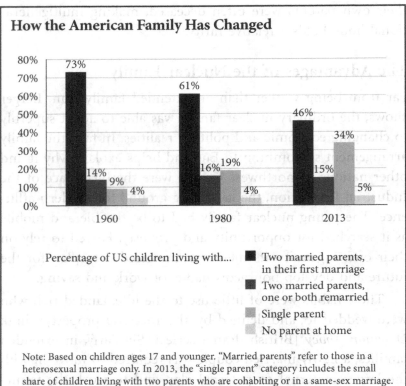

How the American Family Has Changed

Percentage of US children living with...

- ■ Two married parents, in their first marriage
- ■ Two married parents, one or both remarried
- ■ Single parent
- ■ No parent at home

Note: Based on children ages 17 and younger. "Married parents" refer to those in a heterosexual marriage only. In 2013, the "single parent" category includes the small share of children living with two parents who are cohabiting or in a same-sex marriage. Data on same-sex marriage and cohabitation are not available for earlier years.

Source: Pew Research Center analysis of 1960 and 1980 Decennial Census (1% IPUMS) and 2013 American Community Survey (1% IPUMS).

TAKEN FROM: Gretchen Livingston, "Less than Half of U.S. Kids Today Live in a 'Traditional' Family," Pew Research Center, December 22, 2014.

troduced by the Industrial Revolution, which would eventually create an urbanized middle class.

"The Family's Great Educational Mission"

Over time, with the increasing complexity of the labor market and the arrival of mass schooling, forward-thinking, child-centered parents were best equipped to organize themselves around what Berger calls "the family's great educational mission." Extended and clan families under the control of an older generation would be less adaptive since grandparents were more likely to bring up baby the old-fashioned way; larger families, meanwhile, tended to encourage older children to take charge of their younger siblings.

So how does all of this help us understand today's debates about married couple vs. single-parent families? Researchers find that children growing up with two married parents are more likely to develop "soft skills" like self-control and perseverance that are more crucial than ever to school and labor-market success. Some of this could be chalked up to the logistical problems faced by a single parent.

Attention to the Next Generation

But if we follow the logic of Berger's history, another explanation presents itself: The children of married couples are internalizing their parents' bourgeois aspirations and child-centeredness, both of which lie deep in the bones of the institution they have chosen to enter. Contemporary parents continue to marry late—at least those who do marry—and only after they are equipped to teach their kids the skills that they themselves have already learned. Their parenting style can be described as "concerted cultivation": They devote great time and attention to developing their children's skills. Single parents tend to be younger, less educated, and more inclined to believe in the child's "natural growth," to use another of Annette Lareau's terms.

Helicopter parents with their obsessive interest in their children's physical, emotional, and cognitive development are the latest, if occasionally absurd, personification of values with strong historical roots. But, as it has for centuries now, their child-centeredness and future-oriented planning appears to be paying off.

> "In spite of our exquisite tolerance for
> all kinds of lifestyles, we have a wildly
> outdated but strangely pervasive idea
> that single motherhood is worse for
> children, somehow a compromise, a
> flawed venture, a grave psychological
> blow to be overcome, our enlightened
> modern version of shame."

Traditional Ideas of Family Are Outdated and Must Evolve to Be Relevant in Modern Society

Katie Roiphe

Katie Roiphe is a journalist and an author. In the following viewpoint, she argues that crude stereotypes of single mothers have distorted many people's perspectives on single-parent families. Roiphe says that narrow and often oppressive ideas of what families are supposed to be must evolve in today's society. She concedes that single parenthood can be more difficult than parenting in a traditional nuclear family, but it is not necessarily worse for children; in fact, she reviews studies showing that pov-

erty and instability are conditions more harmful to kids than growing up in a single-parent family. Roiphe urges society to be more inclusive of different kinds of families and to be less judgmental of single parents, especially single mothers, for the sake of the children.

As you read, consider the following questions:

1. According to Roiphe, what does James Baldwin say about the opinion of others?

2. How many children in the United Kingdom are growing up in single-parent families, according to the Centre for Social Justice?

3. How many Americans out of ten called single motherhood a "bad thing for society," according to a recent Pew Research Center poll?

I have two different children, with two different fathers, neither of whom we live with and to both of whom we are close. I am not the typical single mother, but then there is no typical single mother any more than there is a typical mother. In fact, it's our unbridled fantasies and crude stereotypes of this "typical single mother" (overweight, short-tempered, popping out babies so that she can snare a council flat) that get in the way of our truly apprehending the richness and variety of thriving families.

The structure of my household is messy, bohemian, warm. If there is anything that currently oppresses the children, it is the idea of the way families are "supposed to be", an idea pushed in picture books, in classrooms, in adults' casual conversation, on children at a surprisingly early age, with surprising aggressiveness.

A "Real Baby"

When I was pregnant, someone who was trying to persuade me not to have the baby said I should wait and have a "regular baby". What he meant, of course, was that I should wait and have a baby in more regular circumstances. But by this point I had seen the feet of the baby on a sonogram, and while he was pacing through my living room making this point, I was thinking: "This *is* a regular baby." His comment stayed with me, though. It evoked the word "bastard"—"Something that is spurious, irregular, inferior or of questionable origin."

Someone said something similar to a friend of mine when she found out that she was pregnant with the child of a man married to someone else. He said she should wait and have a "real baby". And someone else referred to the children her baby's father had with his wife as his "real children". As if her baby were unreal, a figment of her imagination, as if they could wish him away.

Creating a Climate

Small word choices, you might say. How could they possibly matter to any halfway healthy person? But it is in these casual remarks, these throwaway comments, these accidental bursts of honesty and flashes of discomfort that we create a cultural climate; it is here that the judgments persist and reproduce themselves, here that one feels the resistance, the static, the pent-up, residual, pervasive conservatism to which we do not generally own up. Nathaniel Hawthorne called it "the alchemy of quiet malice, by which [we] can concoct a subtle poison from ordinary trifles".

At lunch one day, I am talking to an editor about how I am thinking of writing about single mothers and the subtle and not-so-subtle forms our moralism towards them takes. He says, "That's a good idea. And I say that as a guy who looks at single women and thinks, 'What's wrong with her? How did she screw up?'"

One day, one of my colleagues, noticing that I was pregnant with my second child, ducked into my office and said,

"You really do whatever you want." He meant this as some variety of compliment, and I took it as such, but I was beginning to get the sense that other people were looking at me and thinking the same thing: It seemed to some as if I were getting away with something, as if I were not paying the usual price, and if the usual price was takeaway Thai food and a video with your husband on a Saturday night, then I was not, in fact, paying that price. James Baldwin wrote, "He can face in your life only what he can face in his own." And I imagine, if you are feeling restless or thwarted in your marriage, if you have created an orderly, warm home for your child at a certain slight cost to your own freedom or momentum, you might look at me, or someone else like me, and think I am not making the usual sacrifices. (I may be making other sacrifices, but that is not part of this calculation or judgment.)

Another Way of Living as a Family

I am quite prepared to believe that in a house with two parents, there is generally a little more balance, a healthy divide between adult culture and child culture, a comfortable diffusion of affection. On my son Leo's first birthday, his seven-year-old sister, Violet, wrote him a poem that ended with the lines, "Even if you get a wife, I'll always be the love of your life." And when her father left when she was a little under three, she said, "Mama, it's like you and I are married." This would fairly accurately reflect the atmospherics of our house: a little too much love, you might tactfully say.

But I have to confess that I like the crazy intensity, the fierceness of the attachment, the too-muchness of it. In my heart of hearts, I don't really think "healthy" is better. I think there are some rogue advantages to the unhealthy, unbalanced environment, to the other way of doing things.

Which is not to gloss over the fact that being the only adult in a house with children can be really, really hard. There were times in the first few years of Leo's life where I wished the world would stop spinning on its axis, so I could step off and take a rest.

Moralistic Approach to Single Moms

There is no doubt that single motherhood can be more difficult than other kinds of motherhood. In France, the response to that added difficulty is to give single mothers preferential access to excellent day care. In the UK [United Kingdom], the response seems to be to make alterations to the benefits, tax rates and child-care credits that compound that difficulty; and in the US, the response is moralism disguised as concern, and sometimes just plain moralism.

At the Republican convention last year [2012], former presidential candidate Mitt Romney thought it would be an accurate assessment of reality to blame the rise in violent crime on single mothers. I would be tempted to think of this as a shimmering manifestation of American puritanism, but I notice it in the UK, too. Earlier this month [June 2013], a study by the Centre for Social Justice, a right-wing think tank, warned of a "tsunami" of family breakdown when it found that more than 1m [million] children in the UK are growing up without a father at home. Then there are the furious attacks in newspapers on women who have children by more than one father; women such as Ulrika Jonsson, who was nicknamed "4 x 4" a few years ago, and Kate Winslet, criticised this month for announcing her third pregnancy with a third different father. The *Telegraph* berated her for "disastrous choices", asking, "Has bitter experience (your offspring's, if not yours) taught you nothing?" And continued: "The fallout for the little human beings you've brought into the world is too awful to contemplate." A cooler mind might wonder how the writer could possibly know what goes on in Winslet's children's minds, and whether they are not, in fact, thriving, but cooler minds don't worry as much about other people's private lives.

The Case of J.K. Rowling

J.K. Rowling, one of the world's most spectacularly productive single mothers, addressed this sort of thinking in an article for the *Times* in 2010: "Women like me . . . were, according to popular myth, a prime cause of social breakdown, and in it for all we could get: free money, state-funded accommodation, an easy life." She went on to say, "Between 1993 and 1997, I did the job of two parents, qualified and then worked as a secondary school teacher, wrote one and a half novels and did the planning for a further five. For a while, I was clinically depressed. To be told, over and over again, that I was feckless, lazy—even immoral—did not help."

An Outdated Term

The idea of "single mothers" may itself be the convenient fiction of a fundamentally conservative society. In fact, like Rowling, women move in and out of singleness, married parents break apart, couples live together without marrying, parents die, romantic attachments form and dissolve. Which is to say, the "us" and "them" tenor of the cultural conversation arises from prevailing fantasies of family life that bear no relation to life on the ground.

In spite of our exquisite tolerance for all kinds of lifestyles, we have a wildly outdated but strangely pervasive idea that single motherhood is worse for children, somehow a compromise, a flawed venture, a grave psychological blow to be overcome, our enlightened modern version of shame. It malingers, this idea; it affects us still.

I have noticed that single mothers, or mothers with children from different fathers, seem to do an awful lot of apologising ("I didn't do it on purpose"; "I thought he might stay"; "I think the baby is doing OK. Obviously it would be better if there were a more stable family situation . . ."). There is a sense that you have to explain yourself in a way that almost no one has to anymore, because even the progressive world is operating on a pretty appalling, almost unthinking level of prejudice on this one particular issue. Specifically, people would like to hear that you did not arrange your life in this chaotic manner on purpose, and that you are not enjoying yourself too much, and that you realise your way of doing things is far inferior to the conventional way and possibly blazingly destructive to your children.

Blaming Single Mothers

In America, a recent Pew [Research Center] poll on attitudes toward family structure showed that there is higher tolerance for gay couples raising children than there is for single mothers, with nearly seven in 10 Americans calling single motherhood a "bad thing for society". This in spite of the fact that two of the most popular presidents in recent memory, [Barack] Obama and [Bill] Clinton, were the sons of single mothers. And the fact that currently in America 53% of babies born to women under the age of 30 are born to single mothers; which is to say that most babies born to women under 30 are "bad for society". Our ideas about these things, to say the least, have not caught up with the way we are actually living.

To support the basic notion that single mothers are irresponsible and dangerous to the general order of things, people often like to refer darkly to "studies". To me, these sorts of studies are suspect because they tend to collapse the nuance of true, lived experience and because people lie to themselves and others. (One of these studies, for instance, in order to measure emotional distress, asks teenagers to record how many times in a week "you felt lonely". Is there a teenager on Earth who is a reliable narrator of her inner life? And can anyone of any age quantify how many times in a week they have felt lonely?)

The Role of Financial Instability

However, studies such as those done by the Princeton [University] sociologist Sara McLanahan, who is one of the foremost authorities on single motherhood and its effect on children, make the case that conditions such as poverty and instability, which frequently accompany single-mother households, increase the chances that the children involved will experience various troubles later in life. But there is no evidence that, without those conditions, the pure, pared-down state of single motherhood is itself harmful to children.

McLanahan's studies, and many like them, reveal that the main risks associated with single motherhood arise from financial insecurity, and to a lesser extent particular romantic patterns of the mother—namely introducing lots of boyfriends into children's lives. What the studies very clearly don't show is that longing for a married father at the breakfast table injures children.

And, of course, what these oft-quoted studies don't measure is what happens when there is simmering anger in the home, or unhappy or airless marriages, relationships wilting or faltering, subterranean tensions, what happens when everyone is bored.

In fact, as I learned when I talked to her, McLanahan's findings suggest that a two-parent, financially stable home with stress and conflict would be more destructive to children than a one-parent, financially stable home without stress and conflict. In other words, our notion that "studies show" a single-parent home is categorically worse for children is wrong.

Different Kinds of Family

By now, I have spent so long outside conventional family life that sometimes when I spend an afternoon with married friends and their children, their way of life seems exotic to me. The best way I can describe this is the feeling of being in a foreign country where you notice the bread is good and the coffee is excellent but you are not exactly thinking of giving it all up and living there.

The Changing American Household

- Sixty-six percent of households in 2012 were family households, down from 81 percent in 1970.
- Between 1970 and 2012, the share of households that were married couples with children under 18 halved from 40 percent to 20 percent.
- The proportion of one-person households increased by 10 percentage points between 1970 and 2012, from 17 percent to 27 percent.
- Between 1970 and 2012, the average number of people per household declined from 3.1 to 2.6.

Jonathan Vespa, Jamie M. Lewis, and Rose M. Kreider,
"America's Families and Living Arrangements: 2012,"
US Census Bureau, August 2013.

When my son was two, he referred to his sister's father as "my Harry". He would say, "My Harry is coming!" It seems to me that this exuberant, unorthodox use of pronoun gets at the conjuring, the act of creation, the interesting magic trick at the centre of the whole venture: His family will be what he makes it.

I notice people often find little ways of telling me that this is not the real thing. But is it necessarily worse than the real thing? Is the physical presence of a man in the home truly as transfiguring, as magical, as necessary as people seem to think? One could argue that a well-loved child is a well-loved child. Many people have said to me over the years some variation of, "He needs a man in the house." But does he? It seems to me a little narrow-minded or overly literal to think that love has to come from two parents under one roof, like water from hot and cold taps.

Stretching the Definition

When it comes time for Leo's class to study "families", I worry about how his three-year-old mind will process his family. I don't want him to feel like an outsider in a preschool of married, heterosexual families. We've talked about how there are all different kinds of families, but his world does not reflect that conversation.

When it's time to put cutout silhouettes of family members on the wall, the other children in Leo's preschool class put two parents and two, sometimes three children. Leo puts cutouts of himself, his sister, me, his father, his sister's father and his beloved babysitter, who has been with us since his sister was born 10 years ago. His teacher told me that when he did this, the other children started clamouring, "Wait, my babysitter is my family, too." "What about my grandfather? He takes care of me twice a week."

The wall got cluttered with rogue silhouettes, in bright colours, and I thought, we'll take our progress, paper cutout by paper cutout.

> "Recognition of marriage serves the ends
> of limited government more effectively,
> less intrusively, and at less cost than
> does picking up the pieces from a shat-
> tered marriage culture."

The Breakdown of Marriage
Norms Hurts Society

Ryan T. Anderson

*Ryan T. Anderson is a fellow at the Heritage Foundation. In the
following viewpoint, he observes that a number of major cultural
trends have undermined traditional marriage norms in recent
decades, including the prevalence of no-fault divorce and attempts to redefine marriage to fit a variety of different relationships. Anderson argues that serious social costs result from the
breakdown of marriage norms in American society, including the
increase in single-parent families. He claims that single-parent
families lead to higher rates of poverty, delinquency, drug abuse,
and incarceration, as well as lower educational achievement for
children brought up in such families. In addition, studies show
that single-parent families cost taxpayers billions of dollars every
year to address these social costs. Therefore, it is essential for so-*

ciety to oppose ongoing attempts to redefine marriage and support the traditional nuclear family in the interests of society as a whole.

As you read, consider the following questions:

1. According to Anderson, when was the term "throuple" introduced to the American public?

2. In the author's estimation, how much does marriage reduce the probability of child poverty?

3. According to a 2008 study, how much does divorce and unwed childbearing cost US taxpayers every year?

M arriage plays a fundamental role in civil society because it is characterized by sexual complementarity, monogamy, exclusivity, and permanence. These marriage norms encourage men and women to commit permanently and exclusively to each other and take responsibility for their children.

In recent decades, a revisionist view of marriage has eroded these norms. No-fault divorce was the first major trend to undermine a strong marriage culture. Now the effort to redefine marriage away from male-female complementarity has gone even further in abandoning the central characteristics of the institution. But if the law redefines marriage to say the male-female aspect is arbitrary, what principle will be left to retain monogamy, sexual exclusivity, or the expectation of permanency? Such developments will have high social costs.

The New Language of Marriage

New terms have even been coined to describe this new outlook on marriage. Here are some examples.

"Monogamish." A 2011 *New York Times* profile of gay activist Dan Savage, headlined "Married, with Infidelities," intro-

duced Americans to the term *monogamish*—relationships where partners would allow sexual infidelity provided they were honest about it.

The article explained: "Savage says a more flexible attitude within marriage may be just what the straight community needs." After all, the story added, sexual exclusivity "gives people unrealistic expectations of themselves and their partners." Rather than strive for faithfulness to one spouse, advocates argue for allowing marriage to be sexually open.

Polyamory and "Throuple." If marriage can be redefined to be sexually open, why should it be limited to two people in the first place? The liberal online journal *Salon* in August 2013 posted a woman's account of her shared life with a husband, boyfriend, and daughter under the headline "My Two Husbands." The subhead: "Everyone wants to know how my polyamorous family works. You'd be surprised how normal we really are."

A certain type of polyamorous relationship has even motivated advocates to create the word *throuple*, which is similar to "couple" but with three people. The word appeared in a 2012 article in *New York Magazine* that described a specific "throuple" this way:

Their throuplehood is more or less a permanent domestic arrangement. The three men work together, raise dogs together, sleep together, miss one another, collect art together, travel together, bring each other glasses of water, and, in general, exemplify a modern, adult relationship.

"Wedlease." The word *wedlease* was introduced in an August 2013 op-ed in the *Washington Post*. Why should marriage be permanent when so little else in life is?, the author wondered. Why not have temporary marriage licenses, as with other contracts? "Why don't we borrow from real estate and create a marital lease?" the author wrote. "Instead of wedlock, a 'wedlease.'" He continues:

Here's how a marital lease could work: Two people commit themselves to marriage for a period of years—one year, five years, 10 years, whatever term suits them. The marital lease could be renewed at the end of the term however many times a couple likes. . . . The messiness of divorce is avoided and the end can be as simple as vacating a rental unit.

The Definition of Marriage

Whatever one thinks about the morality of sexually open marriages, multi-partner marriages, and by-design-temporary marriages, the social costs will run high. The marital norms of monogamy, sexual exclusivity, and permanency make a difference for society. These new words and the reality they reflect undermine public understanding of what marriage is and why it matters for society.

At its most basic level, marriage is about attaching a man and a woman to each other as husband and wife to be father and mother to any children their sexual union produces. When a baby is born, there is always a mother nearby: That is a fact of reproductive biology. The question is whether a father will be involved in the life of that child and, if so, for how long. Marriage increases the odds that a man will be committed to both the children that he helps create and to the woman with whom he does so.

Marriage, rightly understood, brings together the two halves of humanity (male and female) in a monogamous relationship. Husband and wife pledge to each other to be faithful by vows of permanence and exclusivity. Marriage provides children with a relationship with the man and the woman who made them.

If a man does not commit to a woman in a permanent and exclusive relationship, the likelihood of creating fatherless children and fragmented families increases. The more sexual partners a man has, and the shorter lived those relationships are, the greater the chance he creates children with multiple women. His attention and resources thus divided, a long line of consequences unfold for both mother and child, and for society as a whole.

Why Does Marriage Matter?

Marriage is thus a personal relationship that serves a public purpose. According to the best available sociological evidence, children fare best on virtually every examined indicator when reared by their wedded biological parents. Studies that control for other factors, including poverty and even genetics, suggest that children reared in intact homes do best in terms of educational achievement, emotional health, familial and sexual development, and delinquency and incarceration.

The breakdown of marriage most hurts the least well-off. A leading indicator of whether someone will know poverty or prosperity is whether, growing up, he or she knew the love and security of having a married mother and father. Marriage reduces the probability of child poverty by 80 percent.

Marital breakdown harms society as a whole. A Brookings Institution study found that $229 billion in welfare expenditures between 1970 and 1996 can be attributed to the breakdown of the marriage culture and the resulting exacerbation of social ills: teen pregnancy, poverty, crime, drug abuse, and health problems. A 2008 study found that divorce and unwed childbearing cost taxpayers $112 billion each year, and Utah State University scholar David Schramm has estimated that divorce alone costs federal, state, and local governments $33 billion each year.

Recognition of marriage serves the ends of limited government more effectively, less intrusively, and at less cost than does picking up the pieces from a shattered marriage culture.

Someone might object: What does it matter if a small percentage of marriages are open, group, or temporary? Those arguments were made in the no-fault divorce debate in the 1960s, but the introduction of such laws had a dramatic im-

pact. After all, law affects culture. Culture affects beliefs. Beliefs affect actions. The law teaches, and it will shape not just a handful of marriages but the public understanding of what marriage is.

Restoring the Marriage Norms

Ideas and behaviors have consequences. The breakdown of the marriage culture since the 1960s made it possible in this generation to consider redefining marriage in the law to exclude sexual complementarity. And that redefinition may lead to further redefinition.

Indeed, these new concepts make marriage primarily about adult desire, with marriage understood primarily as an intense emotional relationship between (or among) consenting adults. This revisionism comes with significant social costs.

Redefining marriage to say that men and women are interchangeable, that "monogamish" relationships work just as well as monogamous relationships, that "throuples" are the same as couples, and that "wedlease" is preferable to wedlock will only lead to more broken homes, more broken hearts, and more intrusive government. Americans should reject such revisionism and work to restore the essentials that make marriage so important for societal welfare: sexual complementarity, monogamy, exclusivity, and permanency.

> "It is not an exaggeration to say that America's social problems and its economic problems are thoroughly intertwined with the decline of marriage and the rise of single parenting."

Marriage, Parenthood, and Public Policy

Ron Haskins

Ron Haskins is a senior fellow for economic studies and codirector of the Center on Children and Families at the Brookings Institution. In the following viewpoint, he argues that if Americans want to address the growing problem of income inequality, policy makers should address one of its main causes: the rise of single-parent families. Children born outside marriage are more likely to live in poverty, be less educated, and have fewer economic opportunities when they reach adulthood than those raised in two-parent homes. Haskins contends that children are paying the price for the breakdown of the nuclear family. There are also major societal costs associated with the rise of single-parent families. Haskins asserts that government policies cannot solve the problem but can be effective in improving the odds for parents in single-parent homes. (Editor's Note: Charts referenced in the viewpoint have been omitted.)

As you read, consider the following questions:

1. According to Haskins, how far have marriage rates declined among twenty- to twenty-four-year-old Americans from 1970–2010?

2. What percentage of American children in 2010 were living with a single parent at any given time?

3. How many men between the ages of eighteen and thirty-four have less than a high school degree, according to the author?

America has been undergoing profound changes in family composition over the last four decades. In 1970, according to that year's decennial census, 83% of women ages 30 to 34 were married. By 2010, that number had fallen to 57%. This drastic decline in marriage rates has coincided with a steep increase in the non-marital birthrate among all demographic groups, from 11% to almost 41% over the same four decades. In 2010, an astounding 72% of births to African American women were out of wedlock.

These dramatic changes are made all the more significant by the ways in which family composition appears to be related to important social, behavioral, and economic characteristics. Children raised by single parents are more likely to display delinquent and illegal behavior. Daughters raised by single mothers are more likely to engage in early sexual activity and become pregnant; their brothers are twice as likely to spend time in jail as their peers raised by married parents. They are less likely to finish high school or get a college degree. And they are four to five times as likely to live in poverty as are children raised by married parents. These intergenerational trends are prominent among both the causes and effects of America's limited social mobility.

Thus, as the nation confronts the stubborn problems of economic inequality and immobility, the rise in the number of single-parent families matters a great deal. The sexual revolution of the 1960s and '70s paved the way for these massive shifts in family life, and these shifts are now making it more difficult for a huge portion of the current generation to get its fair shot in the land of opportunity.

So what is to be done? Answers are difficult to find, but it's not for lack of trying. Both public and private institutions have attempted over the past four decades to decrease the rate of births to unmarried women, either by providing birth control or abstinence education or by encouraging marriage. The federal government has spent billions of dollars trying to counteract the poverty and other social consequences that follow in the wake of the breakdown of the family.

The results so far have been mixed at best, but they do suggest some patterns. Some kinds of interventions appear to make a modest difference on the margins, while others appear to be almost entirely ineffectual. But analyses of these patterns are too often distorted by ideological commitments on all sides. Given the magnitude of the problem, it is essential that analysts and policy makers come to terms with what our experience can teach us so they can seek to build on what works. It is easy to stand back and say that government can't make families, and it is also surely true. But it is nonetheless apparent that there are some ways that public policy, working together with the institutions of American civil society, can help create the circumstances to better enable families to form.

The Rise of Single Parenting

The shape of the typical American family has changed dramatically over the past four decades, in large part due to a precipitous drop in marriage rates. For almost every demographic group, whether broken down by age, education, or race and ethnicity, marriage rates have declined nearly continuously since 1970. The chart below shows the decline in marriage rates for five age groups from 1970 to 2010.

The decline has been dramatic. Marriage rates for 20- to 24-year-olds, for instance, fell from 61% to 16%, a decline of almost 75% in four decades. This drop in young marriages is not so surprising: The couples who do get married now tend to wait longer to do so than they would have a generation ago. What is more surprising is that the marriage rate for older cohorts has fallen as well. The rate for 35- to 39-year-olds, for instance, declined by 25%, from 83% to 62%. The only exception to the pattern of decline was for women with a college degree or more (not shown in the prior chart). After a modest decline of about 11% between 1970 and 1990, the marriage rate for college-educated women stopped declining and even increased by about 1% between 1990 and 2010.

This decline in marriage rates has coincided with steep increases in non-marital birthrates. As the chart below shows, in the same four decades, the non-marital birthrate for African Americans increased by more than 90%, from 38% to 72%. In 2010, the Hispanic rate was 53%, a 50% increase over 1989 (when data on Hispanic birthrates first began to be collected separately from non-Hispanic whites). The rate for non-Hispanic whites, which stood at 16% in 1989, had increased to 29% by 2010, a larger increase in percentage terms than for any other group over that period.

Throughout the 40-year period from 1970 to 2010, women with less education were always more likely to give birth outside marriage, but by 2010 the differences among educational groups had become enormous. As the chart below shows, a 35-year-old woman with less than a high school degree, for instance, was more than five times as likely to be both never married and a mother than a woman with a bachelor's degree or more.

Taken together, the drop in marriage rates and the increase in non-marital birthrates, combined with the substantial increase in the number of married couples who remain child-less, have resulted in a dramatic shift in the composition of the American family.

In the chart that follows, data from the five decennial cen-suses from 1970 to 2010 are used to divide 35-year-old women living in households into four mutually exclusive groups: mar-ried with children, married without children, single with chil-dren, and single without children. Over the four-decade pe-riod, the percentage of married-with-children households declined by well over a third to just 51%. By contrast, the per-centages of all three other types of households increased: mar-ried without children by 72%, single with children by 122%, and single without children by 165%.

The consequences of these changes in family composition are shouldered in large part by the children of single-parent households. These young people make up a fast-growing share of American children. In 1970, 12% of children lived with a single parent at any given time; over the next 40 years, that number increased by 124%, rising to 27% of children in 2010. Over the course of their childhoods, as many as half of all American children will spend some time in a single-parent household.

The available evidence on what growing up in single-parent households means for children suggests this enormous increase in the number of such households is yielding very troubling consequences. Poverty is perhaps the most harmful of these consequences. According to the Census Bureau, in 2012 the poverty rate among children living with only their mother was 47.2%; by contrast, the poverty rate among chil-dren living with their married parents was 11.1%, meaning that a child living with a single mother was almost *five times* as likely to be poor as a child living with married parents.

One of the most troubling aspects of this trend is the negative effect that poverty has on childhood development, es-pecially among children who are poor in their early years.

Given that the major cause of the rise of single parenting is the increase in non-marital births, it follows that many children in single-parent families experience poverty from the moment of their conception. Research shows that mothers giving birth outside of marriage are less likely to have complete prenatal care and are more likely to have babies with low birth weights and other health problems, all of which disrupt child development.

And a higher likelihood of living in poverty is far from the only challenge faced by children who grow up in single-parent families. Until the 1990s, the scholarly world mostly followed the lead of influential developmental psychologist Mavis Hetherington, who concluded that most of the children of divorce soon recovered from the changes in their households and showed modest if any long-term consequences. But a review of 92 empirical studies by Paul Amato, published in 1991, showed abundant evidence that children from divorced families scored lower on several measures of development than did children living in continuously intact families. Then, in 1994, sociologists Sara McLanahan and Gary Sandefur published *Growing Up with a Single Parent*, after which it was nearly impossible to deny that there were serious costs to single parenting. Based on sophisticated analyses of four nationally representative data sets, McLanahan and Sandefur concluded that "children raised apart from one of their parents are less successful in adulthood than children raised by both parents, and . . . many of their problems result from a loss of income, parental involvement and supervision, and ties to the community."

Since 1994, the literature on the effects of single parenting on children has continued to grow. A partial list of these effects includes an increased likelihood of delinquency; acting out in school or dropping out entirely; teen pregnancy; mental health problems, including suicide; and idleness (no work and no school) as a young adult. Married parents—in part simply because there are two of them—have an easier time being better parents. They spend more time with their children, set clear rules and consequences, talk with their children more often and engage them in back-and-forth dialogue, and provide experiences for them (such as high-quality child care) that are likely to boost their development. All these aspects of parenting minimize the kinds of behavioral issues that are more commonly seen among the children of single parents.

Many of these problems have consequences for future generations. One of the reasons it is so difficult for people born into poor families to lift themselves into the middle class is that the good jobs that pay well are often out of reach for those who grew up in poor neighborhoods. This should not be surprising in an economy dominated by high-tech industries and global business: An increasing share of jobs that pay well require a good education, which is much harder to obtain in failing schools in impoverished neighborhoods. And, regardless of the quality of their schools, children from single-parent families on average complete fewer years of schooling, which is correlated with lower adult earnings. This correlation makes it more likely that the cycle of poverty continues into the next generation.

The negative consequences of the rise in single parenting are not limited to those in single-parent families. The trend affects everyone. There are, of course, the immediate costs imposed on taxpayers to pay for government benefits for impoverished single mothers and their children. Single mothers often receive the earned income tax credit, which can be worth over $6,000 per year for a mother with three or more children, as well as the additional child tax credit, which can be worth up to $1,000 per year for each child. Female-headed families are also more likely than married-couple families to receive other welfare benefits such as housing, food stamps, medical care, and other benefits which can be worth several thousand dollars a year.

More important, however, is the human capital lost. Children raised by single parents tend to perform more poorly in school, and this fact appears to be one reason why America's children are falling seriously behind students from other countries in educational achievement. The most recent data from the Programme for International Student Assessment show that American children rank 21st in reading and 31st in math. Equally disturbing, the Organisation for Economic Cooperation and Development has recently published a comprehensive assessment of proficiency in adult literacy, numeracy, and problem-solving across 24 nations. The U.S. was near the bottom in almost every category. For example, 9.1% of American adults scored below the most basic level of numeracy compared to 3.1% of Finnish, 1.7% of Czech, and 1.2% of Japanese adults. The skills assessed by the survey are closely related to adult earnings. Of course, single parenting is not the sole reason American children and adults fare so poorly on international comparisons. But the evidence points unambiguously to the conclusion that single parenting is one factor that accounts for the poor performance of the nation's children.

Many of the problems we associate with failures of American economic policy—especially the persistence of a high poverty rate despite the billions of dollars a year we spend on relief efforts—can also be attributed to family breakdown. Indeed, it is not an exaggeration to say that America's social problems and its economic problems are thoroughly intertwined with the decline of marriage and the rise of single parenting.

Can Anything Be Done?

As the rates of single parenthood have risen and the consequences have become clear, all levels of government from local to federal have attempted to implement policies to address the problem but with limited success. These attempts generally fall into four categories: reducing non-marital births, boosting marriage, helping young men become more marriageable, and helping single mothers improve their and their children's lives.

The first class of policies, those aimed at reducing non-marital births, have met with some success, especially among teens. Teen pregnancy rates have declined almost every year since 1991, and the number of teen births has declined by more than 50% since that time.

It is difficult to identify which specific factors have contributed the most to this success, but several conditions conducive to attacking a national social problem are present in the case of teen pregnancy. There is nearly universal agreement among parents, religious leaders, teachers, and elected officials that teens should not get pregnant. This harmony sends an unambiguous message to teens. Although Republicans and Democrats fight over whether programs should focus on promoting abstinence or birth control, most programs at the local level seem to include both approaches. Teens get a host of messages from their school courses, from community-based organizations, from their parents, and from community leaders that sex can wait and that pregnancy is an especially bad idea.

Surveys show that teens agree with both messages but most of them try to implement only the second—and then indifferently, despite the widespread availability of birth control. As the pregnancy and birthrates show, the situation is improving, but the U.S. still has the highest teen-pregnancy rates of any nation with an advanced economy, and more must be done to address the problem.

The Obama administration has implemented two prevention initiatives that support model programs that have shown strong evidence of success in reducing sexual activity or pregnancy rates among teens. About 200 local programs are now operating under these new funding sources, and the administration has created an elaborate plan for evaluating the local programs. There are also a handful of national organizations, such as the National Campaign to Prevent Teen and Unplanned Pregnancy, which are trying to keep the nation's attention focused on prevention programs and are using social media to reach teens directly.

Though public policies have been successful in reducing teen-pregnancy rates, the problem of non-marital pregnancy is now greatest among adults in their 20s and 30s. Non-marital birthrates among young adults had been increasing steadily until recently, and though the rate is now declining for most age groups, there are still far too many non-marital births.

Fortunately, this is one important social problem against which we have the knowledge and experience to make progress. High-quality modeling research by Georgetown University's Adam Thomas and others shows that additional spending on media campaigns and free coverage of birth control, especially long-acting methods, for low- and moderate-income women would further reduce pregnancy and birthrates and even save money. In addition to this modeling, there is an emerging body of empirical research on the impact of making effective birth control available to young adults.

For example, one recent study of free coverage for long-acting reversible contraceptives (such as implants and intrauterine devices) found that not only did they reduce unintended births but they also reduced abortion rates. Similarly, a recent study from the National Bureau of Economic Research found evidence that "individuals' access to contraceptives increased their children's college completion, labor force participation, wages, and family incomes decades later."

Some Americans of course object to contraception for moral or religious reasons and will therefore object to these programs as well. But for those whose objections have been rooted instead in skepticism about the utility of these approaches or their cost-effectiveness, the evidence of their success is increasingly beyond question. They are not sufficient to stem or reverse the trends of declining family formation, but they can help and should be further implemented.

Promoting Marriage

The second, and perhaps most straightforward, solution to the problem of rising non-marital birthrates is to increase marriage rates. But reversing decades of declining marriage rates is turning out to be exceptionally difficult. Many civic organizations, especially churches, view encouraging marriage as part of their overall mission. Some churches have organized activities to strengthen marriages or help couples survive crises in their relationships. The Catholic Church, in particular, has long insisted on premarital counseling. We have very little reliable data on precisely how many such programs there are and very little evidence regarding their effects on marriage rates or marital satisfaction. We cannot know whether the marriage rate would have been even lower if these civic organizations had not been actively supporting marriage, but it is self-evident that they have not been able to stem the institution's remarkable decline.

Clearly, more evidence and data analysis are called for on this front. But it is also clear that a problem of this scale calls for serious public as well as private action. Apart from providing funds (including tax breaks) for organizations that provide marital counseling and paying for or creating public advertising campaigns about the value of marriage to children and society, however, the federal government has generally not done much to help find a solution to the problem.

The presidency of George W. Bush provided an exception to this rule, as the federal government implemented several marriage-strengthening programs that were executed by state and local organizations, most of them private. These programs provide an initial body of evidence about the possibility of a larger role for public policy in strengthening marriage, and the evidence they provide is decidedly mixed.

The Bush marriage initiative involved several separate strands, including three large intervention studies. One of these studies tested whether marriage education and services would help young, unmarried couples who have babies together improve their relationships and perhaps increase the likelihood that they would marry. Another tried the same approach with married couples, aiming to improve and sustain their marriages. The third studied community-wide programs that adopted a number of strategies simultaneously to bring attention to the advantages of marriage and to strengthen existing marriages at the local level.

The first two initiatives were tested by gold-standard studies; the third was tested by a cleverly designed study that nonetheless involved a less reliable research strategy. In addition to these three initiatives, the Bush administration enacted a grant program that funded 61 healthy-marriage projects at the local level with a total of $75 million per year. Taken together, these four major activities, and others funded through the Department of Health and Human Services, stand as the most thoroughgoing attempt ever by the federal government to have an effect on marital satisfaction and marriage rates.

The results have been disappointing. The community-wide initiative, carried out in three cities, produced virtually no effects in the test cities as compared with three control cities. There have been few high-quality evaluations of the $75 million grant program, so no claims can be made about its effectiveness. (There are now a few ongoing studies of these programs, but none has published results based on rigorous analysis.)

The program for married couples has reported results after 12 months. The effects of the program were small but statistically significant. Couples participating in the program reported modestly higher levels of marital happiness, lower levels of marital distress, slightly more warmth and support for each other, and more positive communication skills.

Spouses in the program group also reported slightly less psychological and physical abuse than control-group couples. The evaluators concluded that the program's positive "short-term effects are small, but they are consistent across a range of outcomes." A follow-up report of the results at 30 months after the program began is due out soon. If the same kinds of effects are still present or are even stronger at 30 months, there may be room for some optimism that married low-income couples can profit from marriage education and support services of the type offered by the Bush program.

The program aimed at helping young couples with an out-of-wedlock baby had some limited success. The test was set up in eight cities, with randomly assigned controls in each site. Six of the sites produced no important effects on the couples, and the Baltimore program showed a few negative ones. But the Oklahoma City test showed a host of positive effects. The Mathematica Policy Research firm conducted studies of the Oklahoma City site and reported that, 15 months after the program began, participating couples were superior to control couples in skills such as resolving disputes, planning finances, expressing positive feelings for their partners, and using good child-rearing techniques.

The effects of the programs for these unmarried couples, however, appear to have been only temporary. When researchers checked again 36 months after the program started, the positive results seen in Oklahoma had dissipated, as had the negative results of the Baltimore test. A program in Florida began to show negative results after three years, but the other test programs showed hardly any effects at any point. Thus, of eight sites, the only good news was from Oklahoma, and most of the encouraging results seen after 15 months had disappeared less than two years later. The couples in the Oklahoma program, however, were 20% more likely to still be together at 36 months than were the control couples in the same study.

The modest success of the Oklahoma City experiment may suggest that something about the program worked. Given the resources invested in the Bush marriage initiative and the programs' quite limited success, however, there is little reason to be optimistic that programs providing marriage education and social services on a large scale will significantly affect marriage rates.

Helping Young Men

The young fathers of the children born out of wedlock present one of the main barriers to more successful marriages and fewer non-marital births. There are currently almost 5.5 million men between the ages of 18 and 34 who have less than a high school degree. Large portions of them grew up in single-parent homes themselves, lived in poverty, and attended failing schools as children. A large percentage of them have prison records. Not surprisingly, poor young women are reluctant to marry them.

These women are, however, willing to have babies with them. After many years of interviews and living in poor neighborhoods, sociologist Kathryn Edin and several research partners have assembled an extensive picture of how these young men are viewed by the young women in their neighborhoods. When asked why they don't want to marry the fathers of their children, the mothers indicated that they didn't trust the young men, that the men didn't work steadily or earn enough money, and that they were too often violent. This description mirrors that of the "cool-pose culture" that Orlando Patterson and other anthropologists apply to men who willingly embrace a lifestyle of hanging out on the streets, working as little as possible, and avoiding binding commitments to family, community, or the mothers of their children. Patterson concludes that the cool-pose culture has evolved to meet current circumstances—especially the difficulty of landing a good job with decent wages—and that no one has figured out a way to break through this culture.

The situation these men face is not fundamentally a result of failed public policies; it is a result of a whole culture of non-marriage, non-work, and serial relationships. It is therefore unlikely that adopting new government policies is going to transform these men into successful husbands and fathers. There are, however, four policy approaches that may help make a difference at the margin.

The first is to address the problem of incarceration. We should start by figuring out ways to avoid putting young men in jail unless they have committed violent offenses. A large number of these young men are incarcerated under mandatory-sentencing laws even for non-violent crimes, and especially for drug-related crimes. Sentencing laws enacted in response to high crime rates in decades past were not irrational or pointless, but it is time for our society to confront their negative consequences and to seek sensible reforms, at both the federal and state levels.

Given the huge proportion of poor young men with prison records, we also need to help these men become productive members of their communities when they get out. There are many programs already in place that attempt to help men who have spent time in prison get jobs and re-integrate into society. One important experimental program in New York City and other locations aims to figure out ways to help young men in juvenile-detention facilities acquire the education, training, counseling, and commitment to personal responsibility they need to avoid subsequent arrests. So far, the research on these programs has been only moderately encouraging. Many of the programs are still in progress, but perhaps the most widely accepted finding is that services, including employment services, for men coming out of prison do not raise employment rates but do reduce recidivism rates. Given this limited but meaningful success with those who have prison records, it seems reasonable to conclude that we should continue and expand research and programs to help young high school dropouts—whether or not they have spent time in jail—stay out of jail and find jobs.

A second, related set of ideas is aimed at finding ways to get these young men better qualified for and committed to employment. The program of this type that has had the most success so far is called career academies, in which students organize into small learning communities to participate in academic and technical education for three or four years during high school. Perhaps the most important aspect of the program is the opportunity students have to gain several years of experience with local employers who provide career-specific learning experiences. An eight-year follow-up of young adults who had participated in career academies showed limited effects on young women but major effects on young men. Young men who had been in the program were about 33% more likely to be married, were about 30% more likely to live with their partners and their children, and earned about $30,000 more over the eight years than the men in the randomized control groups. Expanding the reach of career academies, especially in high-poverty areas, would be a wise investment.

A third policy approach would be to provide young single workers without custody of children with an earnings supplement similar to the earned income tax credit [EITC]. The goals of the program would be to provide an incentive for young men to seek and accept low-wage jobs and to increase their income so they would be more likely to continue working. An experiment testing the effects of this policy is now being implemented in New York City by the research firm MDRC. Young single workers will be eligible for wage supplements of up to $2,000 per year. Their response in terms of employment, earnings, and social relationships will be carefully tracked and compared to randomly assigned controls. If research on the EITC is any indication, this program should increase work rates and earnings and may have additional positive effects on the participants' social lives.

A fourth intriguing policy, again with some evidence of success, would provide job services to fathers who owe child support to help them find steady employment and increase their child-support payments. A program of this type initiated in Texas found that men who had little money to pay child support would, with the help of the program, search for and accept jobs. The study also found that the work rates and child-support payments of these men increased. The federal Department of Health and Human Services has provided funds to a total of seven states (not including Texas) to implement and evaluate similar programs. If the Texas results are replicated, other states should launch employment programs for poor fathers who have difficulty paying child support.

By implementing policies to help poor young men develop the skills they need to break out of a destructive cultural cycle, we can help them become more responsible workers and better fathers. And helping young fathers could help young mothers by giving the men in their lives the tools they need to become responsible husbands and fathers.

Helping Single Mothers

As long as the deep social maladies underlying non-marital childbirth go unaddressed, young single mothers and their children will continue to need help. Today, there are millions of single mothers who do not have the education, skills, or experience necessary to earn enough to escape poverty. So in order to help them provide for their families, the federal and state governments work together to provide cash payments, work subsidies, and a host of work-support benefits.

Since the Great Depression, an evolving set of government welfare programs has helped to meet the basic needs of poor mothers and their children. The most recent manifestation of these programs is a product of the successful 1996 welfare-reform legislation. Instead of a simple cash transfer (as is done with Social Security), the government's major cash-welfare program, Temporary Assistance for Needy Families, is contingent upon work for those who are capable of working. Recipients' wages are then subsidized with an assortment of work-support benefits: cash through the EITC and the additional child tax credit, medical care, food benefits through the Supplemental Nutrition Assistance Program ([SNAP] formerly known as food stamps), and child-care services.

A typical single mother earning, say, $10,000 might receive cash from the EITC and the child tax credit, SNAP benefits, and Medicaid coverage for her children. The children also receive school-lunch and possibly other nutrition benefits. The family might also receive help with child care, although there is not enough money appropriated for all eligible mothers to receive such a subsidy.

The chart below shows the financial impact of these benefits for single mothers in the second income quintile (incomes between about $11,700 and $24,200 in 2010). The market income of these women (most earnings, shown in the bottom line) is increased substantially by the work-support benefits provided by government (as shown in the top line). The chart also shows that both measures of income increased beginning in the mid-1990s when mothers' work rates increased dramatically, primarily due to the work requirements in welfare reform along with a strong economy.

Perhaps the most important feature of this system is that it provides motivation for poor mothers to work because by doing so, even at the low-wage jobs for which most are qualified, they can bring themselves and their children out of poverty. An additional benefit of this system is that a modest number of these mothers prove to have the doggedness and talent to move up the job ladder and increase their earnings over a period of years.

The argument is sometimes made that single mothers are becoming too dependent on government benefits and that only the truly destitute should receive means-tested benefits such as food stamps. But the work-support system has enabled millions of mothers and children to live securely despite limited earnings. Further, many of the mothers who would in the past have been completely dependent upon welfare have now joined the workforce, in large part because of the strict work requirements attached to these benefits.

Politicians should draw a clear distinction between means-tested benefits that go to able-bodied people who do not work and those that go to working people. It is especially important to maintain the benefits for low-income parents living with or supporting children.

Given the current non-marital birthrates and trends, millions of American children over the next several decades will live in families headed by single mothers. Since it is clear that we cannot produce public policies that will give them two married parents, we should do what we can to protect many of these children from the vicissitudes of poverty by continuing and even expanding the nation's system of strong work requirements backed by work-support benefits.

The Limits of Policy

The United States has long been considered the land of opportunity. Americans take particular pride in Horatio Alger stories that seem to prove that anyone willing to work hard enough can make it in our country. That is why reports of rising income inequality and low levels of income mobility have received so much attention; they undermine the ideal of the poor young American able to pull himself up by his bootstraps.

As we have seen, children born out of wedlock are far more likely to live in poverty, and they are far more likely to remain poor as adults. Children raised by two married parents, on the other hand, are not only more likely to have a stable financial situation at home, they also reap the benefits of having more parental investment in their development, better schools, and better neighborhoods. As these patterns reproduce themselves over generations, non-marital childbearing and the poverty that so often accompanies it help to create and sustain two societies within the same nation. Our changing, knowledge-based economy is growing less forgiving of a lack of education, making it hard for young people without college degrees or specialized skills to earn a decent living. And now the last and perhaps most important piece of the traditional American system for building equal opportunity—the married-couple family—is coming apart.

If we want to address the challenges of income inequality and immobility, we must address one of their main causes—non-marital births and single parenting. Maybe stable, married-couple families will never again be the dominant norm, but if so the children who are raised by such traditional families will continue to have yet another advantage over their peers who have minimal contact with their fathers, live in chaotic households, and are exposed to instability at home as their mothers change partners.

Our society and culture will no doubt continue to change, but our children will continue to pay the price for adult decisions about family composition. Public policies cannot ultimately solve this problem, but those that prove themselves capable of ameliorating some of the damage are surely worth pursuing.

> *"Ultimately, what these 'centrist' social policy analysts have to offer is not only denial and rationalization of economic inequality in an 'opportunity society,' but [also] patronizing lectures about responsibility to those who bear the brunt of our collective unwillingness to face poverty and eliminate it."*

Poverty and Income Inequality Hurt Children More than Family Structure

David Green

David Green is a contributor to CounterPunch. *In the following viewpoint, he reviews strong evidence showing that a sharp income inequality is affecting all segments of American society, benefiting only the upper quintile of families. While some liberal institutions have examined the root causes of these concerning trends, several mainstream sources work to deny them. Green identifies the Brookings Institution as one such source that works to rationalize and downplay income inequality through the controversial works of two of its best-known fellows: Ron Haskins and Isabel Sawhill. Green says these authors ignore the evidence that the economic system is rigged to reward the wealthy in favor of lecturing young people to get and stay married. Green questions why centrist and conservative analyses of income inequality focus on the poor and disadvantaged and never address the responsibility of those who benefit from the system.*

As you read, consider the following questions:

1. According to Green, what two liberal think tanks have provided incontrovertible evidence of class warfare, stagnant wages, and increasing inequality and poverty?

2. What mainstream think tank does Green cite as a primary transmitter and ideological shaper of data to support policies that perpetuate long-term economic trends, including income inequality and poverty?

3. What 2012 presidential candidate is cited by Isabel Sawhill as the only one to cite the findings of her work with Ron Haskins on the campaign trail?

Since the recession of 2008, it has become increasingly apparent that for the past four decades the majority of the American population has gotten a raw economic deal. Computer applications and Internet technology have made accessible raw data from the Census [Bureau], the Bureau of Labor Statistics, the Bureau of Economic Analysis, and other government, academic, and think tank sources. These data, honestly conveyed by such liberal think tanks as the Economic Policy Institute and the Center for Economic and Policy Research, provide not just debatable but incontrovertible evidence of class warfare, stagnant wages, increasing inequality and poverty, a transformed and diminished middle class, and an outlandishly wealthy ownership class, especially among financiers. In addition, they find that government policies aid and abet all of the above. At bottom, virtually all of the income and wealth gains resulting from the increased productivity of all workers have accrued to the upper quintile of families, and disproportionately to the one percent or even fewer.

In the midst of hard-core justifications of the wonders and ultimate justice of capitalism and entrepreneurship, one finds—more interestingly, I think—soft-core and "centrist" analysis, rationalization, and ultimately denial of the long-term implications of neoliberal policies. These analyses origi-nate from several data sources, including the University of Michigan's Institute for Social Research and the Pew [Chari-table Trusts] Economic Mobility Project. In passing I recom-mend a much-needed critique by Salvatore Babones of the Michigan/Pew findings [in "Are Americans Better Off than Their Parents?"].

Confronting the Mainstream Narrative

In the mainstream media, the Brookings Institution has been a primary transmitter and ideological shaper of such data, through the policy pronouncements of Isabel Sawhill and Ron Haskins and its somewhat perversely named "Center on Chil-dren and Families." The fact that both have academic pedi-grees and some measure of liberal respectability does not di-minish their trivialization of fundamental issues and their rationalizations for policies that can only perpetuate long-term trends, with dire consequences for the less privileged. In the tradition of Daniel Patrick Moynihan [American politician and sociologist], they continue to use social science to blame the victims of our rigged economic system.

Their primary tactic is to ignore the trends mentioned above and to focus on the allegedly persistent consensus of Americans that economic opportunity and mobility—the "American dream"—is valued more than a broadly egalitarian society. On this basis, massive accumulations of wealth by very few are of literally no interest in comparison to data on marginal intergenerational economic mobility and the behav-

Income Inequality as a Defining Challenge

I believe this is the defining challenge of our time: making sure our economy works for every working American. It's why I ran for president. It was at the center of last year's campaign. It drives everything I do in this office. And I know I've raised this issue before, and some will ask why I raise the issue again right now. I do it because the outcomes of the debates we're having right now—whether it's health care, or the budget, or reforming our housing and financial systems—all these things will have real, practical implications for every American. And I am convinced that the decisions we make on these issues over the next few years will determine whether or not our children will grow up in an America where opportunity is real.

Now, the premise that we're all created equal is the opening line in the American story. And while we don't promise equal outcomes, we have strived to deliver equal opportunity—the idea that success doesn't depend on being born into wealth or privilege, it depends on effort and merit. And with every chapter we've added to that story, we've worked hard to put those words into practice.

Barack Obama,
Remarks by the President on Economic Mobility,
December 4, 2013.

iors required to maintain or achieve middle-class status—regardless of the increasingly tenuous conditions of that status, which also are of no interest. Moreover, mimicking the tactics of the more avowedly conservative Heritage Foundation, Haskins egregiously argues that economic inequality itself is overstated: "The seemingly straightforward story of income inequality therefore turns out not to be so simple. It is a tale of subtle hues, not stark contrasts, and some of the most basic claims thrown around in the media turn out to be rather dubious."

Ignoring the Real Issues

On a practical level, Haskins and Sawhill focus on the relationship between formal education and economic outcomes, regardless of slow economic growth, low-paying jobs, and growing student debt, and regardless of the intractable reality that more schooling for more people cannot possibly in and of itself address the structural nature of poverty in relation to our economy, or the stagnation and struggles of the middle class.

In relation to this emphasis on education, young people are advised by Sawhill on how to best avoid staying or becoming poor:

> "In later research, Ron Haskins and I learned that if individuals do just three things—finish high school, work full-time and marry before they have children—their chances of being poor drop from 15 percent to 2 percent. Mitt Romney has cited this research on the campaign trail, but these issues transcend presidential politics. Stronger public support for single-parent families—such as subsidies or tax credits for child care, and the earned income tax credit—is needed, but no government program is likely to reduce child poverty as much as bringing back marriage as the preferable way of raising children."

> "The government has a limited role to play. It can support local programs and nonprofit organizations working to reduce early, unwed childbearing through teen-pregnancy prevention efforts, family planning, greater opportunities for disadvantaged youth or programs to encourage responsible relationships."

69

"But in the end, Dan Quayle was right. Unless the media, parents and other influential leaders celebrate marriage as the best environment for raising children, the new trend—bringing up baby alone—may be irreversible."

Ultimately, what these "centrist" social policy analysts have to offer is not only denial and rationalization of economic inequality in an "opportunity society," but [also] patronizing lectures about responsibility to those who bear the brunt of our collective unwillingness to face poverty and eliminate it. Moreover, they haven't a word to say about the responsibility of those who benefit most handsomely from the desperate status quo and the misery of others.

Why do conservatives need [controversial commentators] Charles Murray and Thomas Sowell when they've got Sawhill and Haskins?

> "Rarely does the public conversation about the changing economic fortunes of Americans and their families touch directly on questions of family structure."

Single-Parent Families Exacerbate Income Inequality

Robert I. Lerman and W. Bradford Wilcox

Robert I. Lerman is a professor of economics at American University and a fellow at the Urban Institute. W. Bradford Wilcox is an author, the director of the National Marriage Project, and an associate professor of sociology at the University of Virginia. In the following viewpoint, the authors examine the role of family structure on the challenge of income inequality, which threatens the economic health of America's middle class. Lerman and Wilcox argue that the falling rates of marriage and the rise of single-parent families are linked to male unemployment, economic stagnation, and income inequality. These problems are exacerbated for less educated Americans. The authors find that married men reap financial benefits and that two-parent families are more likely than one-parent homes to experience eco-

nomic stability. The authors admit that such analyses involve complex interactions but clearly show that marriage and two-parent families are advantageous for a range of important economic outcomes.

As you read, consider the following questions:

1. According to the authors, what American congressman expressed concern about low labor force participation rates among childless adults in their early twenties?

2. What two scholars have highlighted the growing number of unemployed men without college degrees?

3. Do the authors find that the associations found among family structure while growing up, marriage as an adult, and economic outcomes are definitively causal?

In a major address last year [in 2013], President Barack Obama called the "defining challenge of our time" the "growing inequality and lack of upward mobility that has jeopardized middle-class America's basic bargain—that if you work hard, you have a chance to get ahead." Obama is only the most prominent progressive to call attention to the increasingly unequal, and stagnant, character of much of the American economy. The Washington Center for Equitable Growth, the Economic Policy Institute, economists Alan Krueger and Lawrence Mishel, and many others have identified growing economic inequality and wage stagnation as major issues confronting middle- and lower-income Americans and their families.

From conservatives, attention has focused not only on wage stagnation among middle- and lower-income families but also on the declining share of men in the labor force, especially less educated men. This year, speaking at the American Enterprise Institute, Congressman Paul Ryan expressed concern about "very low labor force participation rates" among childless adults in their early 20s, adding "these are people who are in the prime of their lives that need to get into the workforce." His perspective echoes the work of scholars like Nicholas Eberstadt and Charles Murray, who have highlighted the growing ranks of men without a college degree who do not have a job as what Eberstadt calls an "American flight from work."

The standard portrayals of economic life for ordinary Americans and their families paint a picture of stagnancy, even decline, amidst rising income inequality or joblessness. Progressives tend to apportion blame for this state of affairs to economic shifts—for example, the decline of stable, well-paying manufacturing jobs and the rise of a winner-take-all economy—whereas conservatives are more likely to finger poorly designed public policies—such as Social Security disability benefits—that undercut work.

The Role of Family Structure

But how well do these narratives convey the whole story? Rarely does the public conversation about the changing economic fortunes of Americans and their families touch directly on questions of family structure. This is an important oversight, because changes in family formation and stability are central to the changing economic landscape of American families, the declining economic status of men, and worries about the health of the American dream.

The interactions between the economy and patterns of family life are admittedly complex. Some see the causal chain connecting a bad economy (at least, for less educated workers) to declines in stable married, two-parent families; to poverty and economic insecurity; and subsequently, to poor schooling, job, and family outcomes for children. From this perspective, the appropriate policy focus is on reducing poverty directly, through transfer programs, or indirectly, through enhanced job opportunities.

Social and Political Implications of Economic Inequality

The wealth divide has social and political implications in addition to economic effects. As wealth concentrates, people at the top may develop private replacements for public functions, such as gated communities with private security augmenting public law enforcement, private schools, or private clubs and parks. In Latin America, Africa, Asia, and Russia such privatization of typical public spheres is more common among the highest wealth holders, creating less mixing of different economic classes and less economic diversity in schools, public spaces, and neighborhoods. On a political level, wealth concentration can lead to policy decisions that benefit the wealthy; in countries where private money can be donated to political campaigns, access to wealth may be synonymous with access to political power and policy influence.

"Wealth Divide,"
Global Issues in Context Online Collection, 2015.

An alternative scenario is that declines in the propensity to marry, along with normative shifts in the acceptability of non-marital births and fatherlessness, have led to major declines in stable two-parent families, which in turn have exacerbated problems of poverty, increased inequality, and weakened opportunities for economic mobility. From this perspective, approaches that encourage stable marriages and discourage nonmarital births can be effective in any economy and can lead to new pathways that raise incomes and upward mobility. We find both sets of causal and policy claims compelling.

Complex Interactions

In this report, we describe the role that family structure has played and is playing in the shifting contours of American economic life, both for the nation as a whole and for individual women and men and their families. We explore how the nation's retreat from marriage is linked to growing family inequality, male joblessness, and economic stagnation, especially among the ranks of less educated Americans. We find that men *and* women who hail from an intact family (where both parents are present) are more likely to flourish in the contemporary workplace and to enjoy an "intact-family premium." Likewise, men who marry continue to obtain a "marriage premium" in their earnings. Finally, both men *and* women enjoy a "family premium" in midlife household income if they are raised in an intact family and go on to marry, compared to their unmarried peers from non-intact families who otherwise share a similar background and personal characteristics.

Notwithstanding this report's extensive data analysis, we do not claim that the associations we find among family structure while growing up, marriage as an adult, and economic outcomes are definitively causal. The causal effect of marriage touches on many possible empirical questions, many of which are beyond the scope of this report. Some relate to the causes of higher or lower marriage rates. What happens to economic well-being when, for example, additional marriages are stimulated by financial incentives, attitudes and orientations toward marriage, improved matching, added earnings of men, increased parental responsibility, or changes in laws concerning divorce? Others relate to individual characteristics. Even after netting out the effects of many observed differences among individuals, both marriage and economic well-being may be the result of some third factor, such as unobserved differences in personality or character, like the capacity to delay gratification. While some of the analyses herein control for unobserved initial differences among people, they do not capture changes in a person's overall orientation—say, a desire to settle down—that may lead to marriage and steadier employment. Moreover, most of the evidence in this report is descriptive and does not derive from a causal model. For all these reasons, this report cannot definitively assert that adolescent family structure and adult marital status have a causal impact on individual and family economic well-being.

Furthermore, for some Americans, marriage can be a drag on their family's economic well-being, particularly in cases where a partner is consistently unemployed or when a marriage ends in divorce. This means that marriage and an intact family life are not always associated with better economic fortunes for women, men, children, and families in the United States.

Nevertheless, the evidence is widespread and consistent enough to suggest strong, causal positive roles for being raised in an intact family.

Periodical and Internet Sources Bibliography

The following articles have been selected to supplement the diverse views presented in this chapter.

Annie E. Casey Foundation	"Why Income Inequality Hurts Kids and Families," March 11, 2014.
Gretchen Livingston	"Less than Half of U.S. Kids Today Live in a 'Traditional' Family," Pew Research Center, December 22, 2014.
Robert Maranto and Michael Crouch	"Ignoring an Inequality Culprit: Single-Parent Families," *Wall Street Journal*, April 20, 2014.
Aparna Mathur	"The Biggest Reason for Income Inequality Is Single Parenthood," *Forbes*, November 19, 2014.
Sean McElwee	"The Right's New Charade: Blaming Single Mothers for Inequality," AlterNet, January 17, 2014.
Lawrence Mishel	"Chair Yellen Is Right: Income and Wealth Inequality Hurts Economic Mobility," Economic Policy Institute, October 23, 2014.
National Women's Law Center	"How the Wage Gap Hurts Women and Families," April 2015.
Isabel V. Sawhill	"How Marriage and Divorce Impact Economic Opportunity," Brookings Institution, May 6, 2014.
Jordan Weissmann	"Don't Let Anyone Blame Single Mothers for Economic Inequality," *Slate*, October 28, 2014.
Andrew Yarrow	"How Low Wages Hurt Families and Perpetuate Poverty," Oxfam America, April 7, 2015.

OPPOSING
VIEWPOINTS®
SERIES

CHAPTER 2

What Challenges Do Single-Parent Families Face?

Chapter Preface

According to a 2013 Pew Research Center analysis of US census data, single men make up a growing share of single-parent households in the United States. In 2011, 2.6 million households were run by a single father; in comparison, more than 8.6 million households were headed by single mothers. Since 1960, the number of single-father households has increased by 900 percent. That means that nearly one out of four single-parent families in America today is headed by a single father.

The rising trend of single-father households is relatively recent in the United States and can be traced back to legal reforms regarding child custody laws in the late twentieth century. Until that point, US courts usually opted to rule in the "best interest of the child," which largely meant that the child would live with the mother, but the father would have substantial visitation rights and have a say in all major decisions regarding the child.

After Oregon and a number of other states adopted a "joint parenting" policy, however, the number of single-father households began to increase. The intention of joint parenting policies were designed to give both parents equal time with their children and encouraged collaborative decision making on major parenting issues. In reality, the new policies were empowering men to ask for sole custody and make the case that they were the better option when it came to providing a home for their children. Joint parenting policies led parents and legal authorities to question accepted ideas about custodial arrangements and entertain the idea that men could be the better option when it came to child custody arrangements.

These changes were part of a larger men's movement, which originated largely as a reaction to the successes of the feminist movement of the 1960s and 1970s. Many men's rights activists believe that feminism blames and belittles men and is directly responsible for policies that discriminate against men in the workplace, at home, and in society at large. Specific issues that have generated men's rights activism are advocacy for biological fathers in baby adoption cases; legal support for men accused of domestic violence; and the push for reform of current sexual harassment policies in the workplace.

The most successful aspect of the men's rights movement has been the support of fathers' rights, which developed to protect the rights of men in divorce and child custody cases. The goal was to push for more states to adopt joint parenting policies and confront discrimination against men because of a prevailing gender bias in the American child custody system. Fathers' rights advocates argued that the court system should recognize that children need equal time with both parents, an idea that was truly in the best interest of the child.

Critics of the movement, however, deny that there is any credible evidence that there is a judicial bias against men in child custody cases. They contend that in many cases, men do not want sole or joint custody of their children and agree with the court system that the best place for children is with the mother.

The growing power of the fathers' rights movement was integral to questioning the legal status quo regarding child custody in the 1970s and 1980s and the rise of single-father households in the twenty-first century. This increase in the number of single-father households and the issues they face is one of the subjects explored in the following chapter, which addresses the challenges of single parenthood. Other viewpoints included in the chapter consider the double standard in single parenting, the societal attitude toward single parents, and the need for male role models for children raised in households headed by single mothers.

> *"Single fatherhood is often seen as something done as a choice by honorable men, and single motherhood as something done by women who have made bad decisions and have no other option."*

There Is a Double Standard in Single Parenting

Ellen Friedrichs

Ellen Friedrichs is an educator and a contributor to Everyday Feminism. *In the following viewpoint, she reviews research that shows that many people have a double standard regarding single-parent families. Recent studies find that a majority of people believe that single dads are honorable and are single parents by choice while single mothers are irresponsible and neglectful and are single parents because of their own failures. Friedrichs explores the consequences of this double standard, which results in single mothers being discriminated against and in some cases persecuted by society and the legal system, and she identifies several ways to address this damaging double standard.*

As you read, consider the following questions:

1. According to Friedrichs, what happened to Shanesha Taylor, a single mom in Arizona?

2. According to a 2013 Pew Research Center survey, what percentage of single moms are living in poverty?

3. What percentage of single-parent households are headed by women, according to a 2013 Pew survey?

Recently, I was gossiping with my neighbor about a mutual friend whose wife had moved out, making him the primary parent to their two- and four-year-old children.

"He's been pretty amazing," I said. *"She even took the car, so he brings the kids to day care on the bus. Then he takes the train to work. He's lucky if he even gets to play basketball once a week. And you know how much he loves his league."*

Later, I reflected on the conversation.

Despite also being a car-less, transit-using single parent who can't remember the last time I had a regular weekly recreational activity not related to the eight-and-under set, I found myself marveling at this friend's sacrifices. Then I found myself annoyed that I had slipped into such a typical line of thought.

And if the research is to be believed, it's not only typical to assume that single dads are doing something heroic, but it's just as typical to think that single moms are doing just the opposite.

What the Research Says

Two separate 2012 studies published in the *Journal of Feminist Family Therapy* confirmed that many people put single dads on a pedestal while hyper-policing single moms.

In the first study, "Negative Perceptions of Never-Married Custodial Single Mothers and Fathers: Applications of a Gender Analysis for Family Therapists," authors Amanda [R.]

Haire and Christi [R.] McGeorge determined that many of the beliefs about single parents stem from the view that single fathers have admirably risen to the challenge of parenting by choice, while single mothers are assumed to be parenting out of a necessity resulting from bad judgment, accidental pregnancy, or the failure to maintain a relationship.

The researchers also determined that negative views about single motherhood tend to stem from a conviction that there is something inherently wrong or damaged about a single mother as a person.

Notably, descriptions of single moms given by the study's respondents included the beliefs that this group of parents were neglectful, irresponsible, immature, stressed out, depressed, prone to making bad choices, promiscuous, hopeless, and/or insecure.

Single fathers, on the other hand, were perceived by those surveyed as individuals in a challenging situation who had to worry about complications of solo parenting like paying child support, finding child care, and balancing their dating life with raising kids. Not exactly the personal character flaws attributed to the moms!

In the second paper, "Attitudes Toward Never-Married Single Mothers and Fathers: Does Gender Matter?," researcher Sarah [L.] DeJean and colleagues found that when given a fictional narrative about single parents, identical save for the gender of the subject, study participants were more judgmental of the mothers in the story than they were of the fathers.

Indeed, subjects rated mothers as "less secure, less fortunate, less responsible, less satisfied with life, less moral, less reputable, less of a good parent, and less economically advantaged" when compared to the ratings of the single father, despite the fact the only difference in the vignettes were names and pronouns.

Negative Views Lead to Real-Life Risks for Moms

The effects of such beliefs don't just mean we fawn over single dads and tut-tut over single moms. What we have seen all too often is cases where single moms have either been arrested, faced criminal child endangerment charges, or lost custody of their children for what has been termed child neglect.

In the last few months alone, there has been coverage of a number of moms in these situations.

One example was Shanesha Taylor, a single mom in Arizona who lost custody of her toddler and six-month-old after babysitting fell through and she was forced to leave them in a car for 45 minutes while she had a much-needed job interview.

There was also Debra Harrell, a working mom who spent the night in jail, lost custody of her daughter for over two weeks, and could face ten years in prison after it was discovered that she had let her nine-year-old play in a local park with other children while she worked her shift at McDonald's.

And, of course, in one of the most horrifying cases from the last few years, a Georgia single mom, Raquel Nelson, spent years fighting charges in the tragic death of her son. The boy was killed by a drunk driver after the mom of three jaywalked with her kids since the closest crosswalk was one-third of a mile away from where a city bus dropped the family off after grocery shopping.

Each of these cases—*and they are just the tip of the iceberg*—involved economically disadvantaged, black single moms trying to take care of their kids with very limited means.

While not all moms in these situations are black, a disproportionate number are. In part, that is because if there are negative stereotypes about single moms in general, the promiscuous-black-single-mom-welfare-queen myth makes things exponentially harder for single moms of color, who may be judged through an even narrower lens than are their white single-mom counterparts. That's what we call "intersectional oppression."

The Poverty Disparity

So why don't we hear more about desperate single dads putting their kids in these sorts of situations?

It's not that single dads don't get into trouble with the law, but Google "single dad child neglect charges" and what you get is a staggering number of stories of physical child abuse, not situations involving lost custody or criminal charges for what are often very questionable definitions of neglect.

As many have argued, when charges arise under these circumstances, the real demon is poverty. And poverty is far more likely to affect single moms than dads.

As a 2013 Pew [Research Center] survey found, almost twice as many single moms are living in poverty than are single dads: 24% of single dads versus 43% of single moms.

Combine this with the fact that there are simply fewer single dads out there (another 2013 Pew survey found that 76% of single-parent households are headed by women), and that those who do head families often get a free pass based on our intrinsic belief in the valor of the single dad, and what you get is far more moms being forced into impossible situations than dads.

What We Can Do

A lot of us still hold tight to deeply gendered beliefs about men's and women's roles when it comes to child-rearing.

Understanding that these are socially created views and not biologically determined truths can help us tackle the stigma and dangers single moms face and can help create an environment where more men feel competent at parenting and supported as single dads.

Here are a few other things we can do:

The Stigma Against Divorced Women

Despite its widespread legalization, divorce often comes with the price of social stigma in many cultures. Divorced women, in particular, are viewed negatively. Divorced Muslim women tend to be seen as bad parents and wives in their societies. In India, divorced women have great difficulty remarrying and tend to be viewed more harshly than men, even when they had been physically abused by their husbands. Divorced Indian women are often compelled to move in with their parents or siblings, performing menial tasks and lowering the family's overall status in society. In the Western world and industrialized nations, however, the stigma is fading. Between 1985 and 2004, the rate of divorces between couples that have been married more than twenty years doubled in Japan. Currently, 260,000 couples divorce in Japan every year, 70 percent of these divorces being initiated by women.

"*Divorce,*" Global Issues in Context Online Collection, *2015.*

1. Strive for Gender Parity in Our General Parenting Expectations

As a society, we continue to have overall lower expectations for fathers than for mothers.

The result is that mothers continue to be viewed more critically than fathers, who are often given credit for simply showing up.

Speak up when you notice people commenting on how awesome it is that a dad is at a playground on a Sunday morning and not sleeping in! Call people out when they talk about a dad "babysitting" his own kid. Neither of those things are anything out of the norm. They are just part of parenting.

Remind women that just as attachment parenting, nursing a child until three and co-sleeping are valid options, so too are the tools of modernity like bottle-feeding, [Kraft microwavable macaroni and cheese], disposable diapers, and cribs and toddler beds, that can help give moms freedom from their kids and can help dads co-parent equally.

2. As Moms, Allow Dads to Thrive

When an opposite-gender couple splits, women often correctly fear that relegating the role of primary parent to the father will find them harshly judged, even if the father would be better equipped for the job.

Don't assume that there is some horrifying backstory if a dad is the primary parent. Unless given real reason to think otherwise, assume that he is competent in his role. Similarly, stop yourself from critiquing a dad's parenting style if you wouldn't do the same to a mom.

3. Demonize Poverty, Not Single Moms

Blaming single moms and not the severe financial disadvantage so many face can have disastrous consequences and has resulted in the recent arrests and the loss of children for a number of mothers.

Work to fight poverty and support programs for parents like parental leave, universal pre-K, and subsidized day care. Back the fight to increase the minimum wage to something livable and get political, for example, by urging Congress to pass the Healthy Families Act, which would provide a national paid leave program, since a lack of paid leave can be devastating to a working single mom.

4. Acknowledge Inherent Biases About Single Parents

Single fatherhood is often seen as something done as a choice by honorable men, and single motherhood as something done by women who have made bad decisions and have no other option.

When we accept this view, we perpetuate harmful myths.

If you would offer to babysit for a single dad because he needs a night out, do the same for a single mom.

5. Admit When Mainstream Thinking Affects Us

As feminists, we need to acknowledge and challenge our own gender biases when it comes to parenting.

Despite knowing it's not true, many of us still secretly think parenting comes more naturally to women than to men.

Work Still to Be Done

When my great-grandmother got divorced in France in 1912, her actions were beyond scandalous. The fact that she became a single mother after the dissolution of her marriage and not as a result of widowhood was almost unheard of, and both she and my grandmother felt the sting of stigma their entire lives.

Luckily, we have moved forward and divorce and the single motherhood that often results are both much more commonplace and also much more accepted than they were a century ago.

But as plenty of single moms can attest, simply being *more* common and *more* accepted, doesn't quite cut it. And really, if we want families to thrive we have to accept that they come in all sorts of configurations and we have to work to support not only those which we think are deserving or noble, but also those whose choices and configuration may look vastly different from our own.

> *"Single parenthood is like drowning and being on fire at the same time and everyone will go on and on about how beautiful the spectacle is—how strong you are, what brave work you're doing, how they could never do something so incredible."*

Single Parenting Is Difficult but Very Satisfying

Kristin Leong

Kristin Leong is an educator and a blogger. In the following viewpoint, she reflects on the numerous challenges that she has faced as a single mother raising her son, including legal and financial issues, a lack of institutional and familial support, and several personal sacrifices. Leong asserts that although motherhood felt like a curse at times, it has been a transformative and satisfying experience. She observes that as her son has gotten older, things have gotten easier, and she feels more successful and secure in her parenting. She advised her friend, who was thinking about single motherhood, to do it despite the financial and personal challenges she will face along the way because it is ultimately worth the personal sacrifice.

As you read, consider the following questions:

1. What was Leong's profession when she got pregnant?

2. In what store did the author's son throw an epic tantrum over a box of tampons?

3. What did the author give her son for his birthday?

When my friend tells me she's thinking about having a baby on her own, my mind flashes immediately to that January morning in 2011 when, as I just settled my eighth graders into a rare calm, my son's father burst into my classroom with a video camera, sloppy drunk, slurring demands about my son's whereabouts. It was my first year teaching. My son was two. Single parenting, I wanted to tell her, is filled with so many unexpected adventures, so many of them horrible. Don't do it. Don't do it. Don't do it. You have no idea what you're getting yourself into.

A Personal Account

I had no idea. I was a nightclub bartender still trying to figure out what to do with my Sarah Lawrence [College] degree when I found out I was pregnant. I also had no idea about my seemingly benign but dopey bartender boyfriend. Although I had known him for years, I never could have imagined the evil and manipulation that lurked inside of him, rearing its drunken head even before getting through those forty weeks of pregnancy. I knew from the start that I would be a single parent and I thought it would be hard but I had done hard things before. If I had known how hideous and consuming everything would have to become before it got better, maybe I would have made different decisions. Maybe not. I was twenty-six. I thought I could do whatever I wanted.

Not that the disaster that ensued could have been anticipated. The war to the legal protections to keep my son relatively safe from his biological father has been fraught with red tape and loopholes that raised the eyebrows of even the most stoic judges and Family Court officials. After that classroom incident the judge told him, *Don't ever do that again.* And then nothing. After my son was returned to me branded all over his body with a nightclub entry stamp that said *SEXY* in bold black ink, the judge said, *That's totally inappropriate.* And then nothing. When my son was left on my doorstep with a grossly swollen and bloody mouth, his arms and legs bloody too, crying, wearing only shorts and no shoes or shirt, at two years old, while his father drove away and then didn't answer calls for three days, the judge said he couldn't determine if the injuries were caused by abuse or neglect. *I'm sorry,* that judge explained, *neglect is not illegal in this state.* I cried in front of him, more shocked than angry, unable to turn around and walk out of the courtroom. *Look at the pictures again. Look. He's just a baby. Please, please, please.* But nothing. The stories go on and on.

Those stories are starting to feel like a long time ago. There are now so many things for which to be grateful. My son just turned six. Despite everything, he is happy and kind and light. There must be so much luck involved. And grit. Finally life doesn't just feel like survival.

Legally things are turning around, slowly, one clause in the parenting plan at a time. A Family Court evaluator here. An arbitrator there. Slowly the people with power to help my son are starting to see what I've known all along—fighting for visitation isn't always about love for the child. Domestic violence and alcoholism lie with charm and persistence that look so much like commitment.

Many Challenges

Motherhood doesn't feel like a Sisyphean [referring to Sisyphus, a figure in Greek mythology condemned to repeat the task of pushing a boulder up a hill, only to have it roll down again] curse all the time anymore either. I remember lying in bed with my son as a toddler holding on to him like a life raft. *What are we going to do. Someone just tell me what to do. I can't do this anymore.* That was back when there was never enough of anything—money, food, work, child care, compassion. And there was teething and toilet training. I had to find a preschool. He's outgrown his shoes already. And grad school! And then he's tantruming in Target over a box of tampons I took away from him and he's screaming with his entire little self that's been passed around, neglected, left on doorsteps, stamped, all of it, and he's screaming with so much pain and desperation that I just let him wail right there in the middle of the aisle while I dared anyone in earshot to say something just so I could scream back, HE GETS TO LET THIS OUT, YOU DON'T KNOW WHAT WE'VE BEEN THROUGH.

I have begun to sweat as I write about that tantrum. My chest feels like it's closing up. I think about his birthday morning. It's a Tuesday, a school day for both of us. I woke him up early to give him his presents wrapped shoddily in pages from a magazine. Two presents. A shark tooth fossil and a stuffed dog. The exact stuffed dog that my grandmother gave him when he was barely walking. Pancake. This dog—it's formally white belly is grey even fresh out of a hot wash, his eyes are scratched off, his fur is matted into gross little spikes—has survived so many moves, so many other fleeting comforts in and out of our lives, and my son loves him with an animal ferocity. I have worried before that he should have outgrown Pancake by now, that this stuffed animal has become some kind of psychological crutch that will make him into a weird grown up one day. Finally, I accepted Pancake for what he is: just love and comfort. Totally unconditional, uncomplicated, reliable. And my son deserves that. Everything in our life is moving under us all the time. For the better. But still. So another Pancake. A backup, not a replacement. In our family we are loyal to the core.

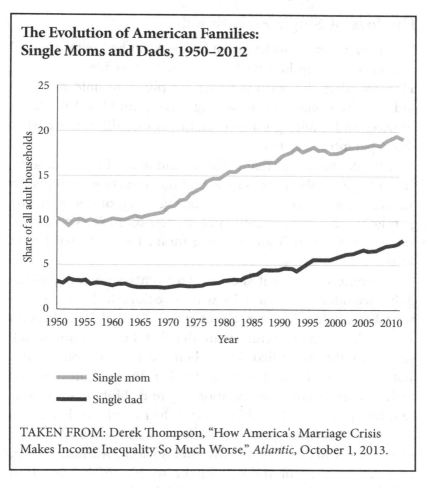

The Evolution of American Families:
Single Moms and Dads, 1950–2012

Single mom

Single dad

TAKEN FROM: Derek Thompson, "How America's Marriage Crisis Makes Income Inequality So Much Worse," *Atlantic*, October 1, 2013.

After he opened his presents he didn't say anything but he moved over to sit on my lap and I held onto him hard, six-something in the morning on a Tuesday, totally awake for this moment even as it passed. He's becoming so cool these days. He tries out sarcasm when he's feeling gutsy. He wrestles me hello and doesn't want to hold my hand across the street anymore. He has clear opinions on sneakers. He's quick to tell me his Lego guys have lasers when I tell him there's no guns allowed. He tells me he has a girlfriend. I'll take all the soft quiet moments that are left.

The Joys of Single Parenthood

The other night he woke up and crawled in bed with me, and instead of walking him back to his room, I let him stay. As he fell back asleep, he reached under my pillow to hold my hand and we stayed like that for a long time. I could feel my heart glowing and swelling outside of my body. All of the clichés about parenting are true.

I think about my friend. She is kind and witty and beautiful and quick. She goes on meditation retreats with nuns on the weekend, when she is not scaring away online dates by getting into her sustainability politics too soon. She's a teacher, too. She will be such an awesome mom. I want to tell her to do it.

I remind myself that she is not a twenty-something nightclub bartender having a baby with a sociopath. I want to tell her what it's like to learn about unconditional love through the shock of experiencing it for the first time. I want to tell her about the unbridled joy of being a part of your child's first shit in the toilet. I want to tell her about being vomited on in the early hours of the morning and thinking only, dear god, just put all of this child's sick into me, please, help him, take away everything that hurts him. I want to tell her about what it feels like to cry, finally, after so long without crying, kneeling in front of the bed in the middle of helping him with his shoes, because I really couldn't take it anymore and then to have him—four years old—bring me Eleanor, a little stuffed elephant, while he took Pancake and sucked his thumb next to me until I got it all out. I want to tell her about how empowering it's been for me to really get my issues together because another human being utterly depends on me and there is no one else, no backup, no breaks, no child care that doesn't come with some kind of strings.

Single parenthood is like drowning and being on fire at the same time and everyone will go on and on about how beautiful the spectacle is—how strong you are, what brave work you're doing, how they could never do something so incredible. And meanwhile you're on fire, you're drowning, and you can't hear them at all, you just keeping thinking I'M DYING I'M DYING I'M DYING. But then you don't die. And your child gets older, starts making it easier on you. They learn to dress themselves. They can feed the dog. They can tell you if your yoga pants are see-through when you bend over. The threat of tantrums no longer looms over every trip to the store. And then sometime around kindergarten their jokes actually start to get funny. Their help around the house starts to actually be helpful. They start to feel like your sidekick and you start to feel like a superhero. You survived all that drowning and fire after all.

Yes, I want to tell her to do it and that I'll help with whatever she needs—she doesn't know yet how much need there will be; it's impossible to imagine the village that children require and then to imagine having an actual child and realizing that that village is just rhetorical fantasy. What to do then? Keep raising that baby. Cry it out whenever you need to—in Target, wherever. Tell your story. As the waters rise and the fire rages on, just tell the story while it's happening, scream it out like a tantrum. It feels good. And then it starts to feel good more and more and one day you wake up and you realize that you've survived the babyhood and the toddlerhood and your child is a person and he is good. And you did that. You get all the credit, you do, even with luck and grit in there too. It's all you and now there is more love in your life than you ever thought you deserved and you are good too because of all of it. Yes, I want to tell her. Do it. Have that baby on your own. It will be horrible and beautiful and the days will be long but the years will fly by and sooner than later you'll look into the face of the human you raised on your own and think, *yes, we did it.* And you might not choose to do it all over again but no, definitely not, you wouldn't change a thing.

> "When I think of the incredibly unreasonable expectations we have on mothers in general, I am shocked."

Single Motherhood Is Demanding

Sash Milne

Sash Milne is a blogger and writer. In the following viewpoint, she elucidates the emotional, physical, and financial challenges associated with being a single mother in today's society. Milne contends that most women do not reveal the truth as to how demanding and draining it really is to be a single parent because women do not want to admit to the outside world that they are having a hard time coping. She confesses that she is often overwhelmed by the responsibilities of single motherhood. Because there is so much cultural ignorance surrounding single motherhood, women in that position also have to deal with crude stereotypes and discrimination. These misconceptions are often amplified by television shows and the media. Milne suggests that it is time that society considers these issues and starts supporting single mothers without judgment.

As you read, consider the following questions:

1. How long does the author estimate that she has been functioning as a single parent as long as her daughter has been alive?

2. What does Milne identify as her own biggest challenge with single parenting?

3. What does the author say society offers single mothers instead of the support they need to raise their children?

My husband had an affair, but long before he did this he made choices that kept him away from us. Right from the very beginning. He chose other people, other events, other places over his family. So even though our relationship only broke down two months ago I've been functioning as a single parent for about eighty percent of the time that Bo has been alive.

Family History

My mother was a single parent. When I was eleven, my parents' marriage ended and my mother became solely responsible for my two younger brothers and [me]. It sunk her into a deep dark hole. She did the best she could for us, but it nearly destroyed her. I didn't understand then, but I do now. I didn't always agree with the choices she made, and I still don't, but I know that everything she did was out of love for us. I knew then that she wasn't coping. And I understand that now, more than I ever wanted to.

Except for women who choose to fall pregnant (via sperm donor or the like) and know right from the beginning that they will be a single parent (and for the record I don't think this makes it any easier really), I don't think there is a single woman on this earth who faces single parenthood without some reluctance. Doing it alone, for most of us, was never the game plan. Relationships fall apart, people die, people fall out of love, people cheat, people move on, people make choices . . . good and bad . . . that affect the course of the lives of everyone around us. We are all intrinsically connected after all.

The Challenges

There is so much to be said about the honest experience of the single parent. There is so much silence surrounding the truth. There are so many things that people are afraid to say. Women so afraid of admitting they aren't coping. Afraid of the judgment that they face. So many women who are terrified to ask for help. Women who are asking for help and not getting it. Women who are struggling financially, emotionally, spiritually but who aren't being heard. So many truths that aren't understood. And therefore, there are so many misrepresentations and the great social prejudice that comes with a great social silence. The attitude that our society has that tends to blame a single mother for her circumstances, I believe, comes from a greater unknowing. An incredible cultural ignorance.

There is a great social prejudice against single mothers. Women who have babies and who leave their husbands. Women who choose to continue a pregnancy even when the paternal father refuses to acknowledge the baby as his responsibility. Women who make great personal sacrifice for the sake of a child. For the well-being of a child. The woman who decides to continue a pregnancy even though the man she is with (or was with) chooses to opt out. The attitude of our society that choosing not to terminate a pregnancy somehow equates to her having sole responsibility for the care of that child makes no sense to me. Because of biology (and society) men have the option of cashing out of a relationship, of a family. They can walk away and continue their lives much like before, without great (financial or emotional) responsibility, sleep deprivation or stress. They can go back to friendships and relationships and family. . . . But the woman (and I say woman here, but this is of course not only the case, single dads experience the same if not greater prejudice at times) is left behind. With a great responsibility, (almost always) a decline in living conditions and lifestyle and, more often than not, no real help.

I don't think anyone can truly appreciate the incredible emotional responsibility that a woman is left with when she becomes a single parent. It is not only the 24-hour-a-day, 7-days-a-week responsibility of the care of a child. It is not only the incredible stress of sole (in many cases) financial responsibly. It's not only the incredible pressure of being the only person to make every choice surrounding a child's care and upbringing and circumstances. It's not just the fact that it is completely and totally unreasonable that our society expects that ONE person, alone and completely without support, can be undeniably patient and giving to a child day in, day out for many, many years. It is insane and it is just not humanly possible. It is all of these things in combination with each other, and so many more.

Time

For me, as a single parent, the biggest challenge with single parenting is *time*. The lack of time is directly related to my own issues of a loss of identity and self-esteem. Issues that I am trying to conquer, trying to overcome, trying to become empowered by, instead of feeling powerless because of. I am a parent for every minute of every day. Even at night when Bo has gone to bed and I have gone to work, sitting at my desk in the spare room, I am still the only parent in the house. I know when she wakes (and she does, often) that it is always me who will go to her. I can't pop out for a trip to the supermarket alone or catch up with friends without a baby or have a long bath or go for a walk because there is no one else for the day-to-day. It is isolating and it is a very displacing feeling. I'm not sure if anyone who has not lived in it could understand the incredible loneliness that comes from being trapped, in isolation, with a small child the only regular company and a lack of adult conversation. *As lovely as my daughter is, and as wonderful a conversationalist [as] she is becoming—we still don't speak the same language.* It's not enough. That is something that people don't truly talk about. About the late nights alone. The frustration with a clingy, needy child that you get no break from. Caring for a sick child alone (and then often sick, yourself). There is so much silence, and in that silence I am sure there are other mothers suffering. Truly suffering with little or no input from outside of the relationship she has with her child. But why can't she speak up? What have we done as a society that has alienated all of us from each other? Where asking for help is seen as a weakness? Where offering help is a last resort?

Sometimes I am overwhelmed by the incredible responsibility that is being a sole parent. I look at Bo and I think, how can I possibly do this, all of this, alone? This isn't what I wanted. I wanted to be with her father. I wanted the happy family. I wanted to be together. To share the load. To share the joy. I wanted to be able to sit on the couch with my husband at the end of the day and laugh about the beautiful things she did, and cry over the frustrations and have him there to hold my hand and help out and love her like I do. Because as hard as it is to not be able to share the challenges . . . it's just as hard not having someone right there to share the joy. The little things, like a kid finally doing a poo after being bunged up for a few days, or eating their whole lunch, or having a proper nap. . . . We want to share these things with someone and let's be honest, no one else cares about those things as much (or if at all) as the parents.

The other night Bo woke at 10 PM and wouldn't go back to sleep so I got her up and snuggled with her on the couch in front of a movie. She was so *beautiful.* She sat eating peanut butter on toast. Licking her fingers and talking to me very se-

Single Mothers and Poverty

Single mothers in all societies are vulnerable to poverty. While the current female president of Chile, Michele Bachelet (1951–), is an unmarried mother, social acceptance of single motherhood in Chile and other Latin American nations is uneven, with greater acceptance in more urbanized areas. Poverty correlates with single motherhood in Costa Rica, for example, where antipoverty efforts in the 1990s and 2000s were diluted by an increase in single-mother households. Single mothers, because of the stress of heading the household, often cannot find or manage full employment. They may settle for part-time or temporary work, which lowers family income and increases poverty rates. In China, single motherhood is a relatively new phenomenon, and one that is penalized under the country's strict population control policies. Establishing residency in a city requires a father, as does registering children for school. These hurdles increase reliance on men, even for women who come from higher socioeconomic groups.

"Women in Poverty,"
Global Issues in Context Online Collection, *2015.*

riously in her own language, every now [and then] pausing and raising her eyebrows at me ... as if to say, *do you understand mama, are you hearing me?* And I would say, *yes of course.* She would then start giggling and shouting at the people on the TV. And it was such a perfect moment. I looked at her and I could see a glimpse of the little girl she is going to be and I wish her dad had been here to see her. To share in the absolute joy that she is. I wish I had someone to truly share those moments with. The moments of pride.

Unfair Expectations

When I think of the incredibly unreasonable expectations we have on mothers in general, I am shocked. Our society pushes for (unreasonable) perfection. Our society expects that mothers should raise these perfect children whilst being essentially isolated from the world. Instead of offering support, we offer judgmental advice, books with parenting "rules" and guidelines that have the potential of stripping mothers of their instinct. And then we add on top of that a mother without the support of a partner, without the small moments of respite that the partnered mother is given. Without the time to find herself. And we turn around and we judge these mothers. Single mothers. We judge them. I know a young single mother who was called the most disgusting names by her own brother because she is without a man. Because she chose to continue her pregnancy and raise her beautiful child alone. Because she didn't have the choice to just "walk away." Because she chose life. We judge women we see alone, wrangling children. The plight of the single parent has become fodder for television shows and sitcoms and jokes . . . what we don't do is offer real, supportive, full assistance. I'm not talking about pensions or money or aid. I'm ashamed (albeit extraordinarily grateful) to have to ask for a handout from the government to survive . . . and I'm sure most people are. I'd prefer to have the facility to raise my child the way (I believe) she deserves to be raised and work enough to make good money to support us without help. But as one person, that is not possible right now; our society doesn't support working options for mothers who want to keep their children with them.

I'm talking about swapping judgement for humanity. Hate for love. Do-it-my-way advice for hands-on help.

Why is it so hard for us as a society to be supportive of our people? Why are we always so quick to judge and so slow to react? When did we become so distant from each other? When did society stop being about community? When did parenthood become more about rules and less about raising good, strong, caring people, together?

Perhaps a little jumbled, but food for thought nonetheless. Even better for discussion.

"What I will share with any man who is just stepping into this new world of single parenting is to take a deep breath and let go of your expectations."

Single Fatherhood Is Difficult

Dave Taylor

Dave Taylor is a blogger and fathers' rights activist. In the following viewpoint, he reflects on the challenges that he has faced as a single father to three children. Taylor maintains that single fatherhood is very difficult, even more difficult than single motherhood, in fact, because men are not raised to be nurturing or empathetic. Therefore, he had to evolve from being strictly a disciplinarian to develop other ways of dealing with his children. Taylor points to poor media portrayals of fatherhood and crass images of masculinity as other hindrances to single fathers. He finds that men don't have many role models to look to when it comes to single parenting. It is vital for new single parents to let go of such stereotypes as well as unrealistic expectations and live in the moment to be the parents their children need. Taylor also suggests that single fathers be sure to cut themselves some slack and to ask for help if they need it.

As you read, consider the following questions:

1. What does the author say was running through his head when he got married eighteen years ago?

2. How old were Taylor's children when he got divorced?

3. What does Taylor say that he learned about single fatherhood?

No one goes to the altar expecting to end up divorced, but it's a distressingly common occurrence nonetheless.

Couples get together with the very best of intentions, full of hopes and dreams, white picket fences, 2.5 kids, or even a penthouse uptown. A life together, a future as a team, and perhaps some little people added to the mix.

That's what was running through my head when I walked up the aisle almost 18 years ago, anxious, teary and excited to take the next step in my life with the woman I loved.

Then we had one, two, three children and somehow bringing tiny little people into the mix didn't make our relationship any easier, didn't help us find a common ground and get along smoothly. Every parent knows this, but you have to find out yourself anyway: having a child is hugely stressful on a relationship.

We tried to make it work. We talked, we tried different approaches to parenting, we worked with counselors, we went to workshops and seminars. But that fateful day came to pass where we just realized that, kids or no kids, we were really not making it as a couple and were both perpetually unhappy and resentful.

So we split up. Theoretically, to have a break from each other, but I could read the writing on the wall and started preparing myself for what ended up being a long, contentious divorce.

Single Parenting Is Hard. Single Fathering Is Even Harder.

I suddenly found myself a single dad, with children who were 10, 6 and 3. And while I'd always been an active, involved dad, it was a completely different experience when I didn't have someone to help out if I was getting frustrated, was tired, not feeling well, or just had a vision of things going one way while they were quite clearly headed in another direction.

Like going from tag-team wrestling to having to take on the other opponent solo. Worse, in a lot of situations, far from "having your back," your ex can be eagerly waiting to point out your failings, digging that knife in just a bit deeper, while telling the children "daddy has issues, but at least you have me."

Let Me Be Blunt. It's Not Easy Being a Single Parent.

I think it's tougher on us men, however, because we aren't raised to nurture and be empathetic. In fact, Western society does its best through a culture of shaming, bullying, crass images of masculinity and dismal media portrayals of fathers to teach us men that we're just not going to be successful parents.

We don't tote babies around when we're little, we aren't the one hired to babysit the twins down the street when we're in our teens; we're instead pushed to physical activities, sports, video games and other activities that emphasize the testosterone factor rather than help us learn how to balance it with the more traditionally "feminine" aspects of humanity.

And so retrospectively, it's no surprise to me that the first year of my single parenthood was damn hard. I had always been the disciplinarian in our household, the one who actually had—and enforced—rules and behaviors. Suddenly life was about a lot more than just being the drill instructor and I didn't know how to handle it. A crying toddler? A grumpy daughter because a boy snubbed her? A boy devastated because he failed to make the winning shot? All new because I couldn't rely on mom to be the sympathetic parent.

It was rocky, and there were definitely moments I look back on with great sadness and disappointment. I could have done better, I could have handled them better. Or perhaps not. Perhaps the journey of man to loving father does require some turbulence along the way.

Interestingly, my ex's household was chaos for years because as a single mom she faced the opposite challenge, that she's wonderfully sympathetic and therefore rarely had rules and certainly hated to enforce them or impose consequences for violations. Her household was a zoo, with no bed times, no meal times, all replaced by lots of mom/kid cuddling and sharing.

Reflections on Single Fatherhood

Time has a way of healing and improving things, and after almost 7 years of flying solo, I've learned a few things about finding the balance between innate male reactions and the need for a child to have a parent who is present, who is tough when needed but who is also sympathetic. Sometimes a hug and a treat are the best response while other occasions require a time out or extra chore.

What I will share with any man who is just stepping into this new world of single parenting is to take a deep breath and let go of your expectations. Parenting really isn't about tomorrow as much as it is about this very moment. Rules are good, but their little hearts, their expectations, their dreams are what it's all about, so pay attention. Listen. Don't "fix" things that don't need fixing. And have fun. It took me years to be able to really just relax and enjoy my children.

And cut yourself slack. It's a tough job, this solo parenting thing. You'll make mistakes, but with positive intention and

love, you'll all make it through. If it's going really poorly?
Reach out and get some help. No shame in that, brother.

> "The growing trend of father absence
> could have grave implications for soci-
> ety, researchers say, because having dad
> around has been linked to important
> developments in a child's physical, emo-
> tional and behavioral health."

Children Need Fathers to Provide Stability and Act as Role Models

Elizabeth Stuart

Elizabeth Stuart is a reporter. In the following viewpoint, she traces the growing trend of "father absence" in the home, finding that American society has been steadily moving away from the institution of marriage since the start of the sexual revolution in the 1960s. Without a strong male role model in the house, children are more likely to end up as juvenile delinquents, school dropouts, or drug addicts and face other challenges. Stuart reports that studies show that households with fathers are more economically stable and produce better educated and socially adjusted children. For these and myriad other reasons, it is crucial for children to have an involved father in the home.

As you read, consider the following questions:

1. According to the US Census Bureau, what percentage of American children are growing up without their biological father?

2. How many unmarried couples does the US Census Bureau identify as raising children together in 2009?

3. According to a Wisconsin Department of Health and Social Services study, what percentage of juvenile delinquents in the state came from a family where the parents never married?

Two stints in prison, rehab and a probation officer failed to inspire Mike DeBoer to give up the drugs. Dirty diapers, peanut butter sandwiches, playing "tickle monster" with a giggly redhead who smiles his daddy's smile—that's what did it.

"My dad wasn't there for me," said DeBoer, 30, a thick, muscular man with a shaved head and five o'clock shadow, pausing to coo at his now-17-month-old son. "There's nothing in the world that's gonna keep me from being there for my little man."

One-third of American children are growing up, as DeBoer did, without their biological father, according to the U.S. Census Bureau. In the past 50 years, the percentage of children who live with two married parents has dropped 22 points. During that same time, the number of babies born to unwed mothers jumped from 5 percent to 40 percent.

The growing trend of father absence could have grave implications for society, researchers say, because having dad around has been linked to important developments in a child's physical, emotional and behavioral health. At the same time, though, research indicates it's not enough just to have a male figure in the home.

Several leading sociologists have labeled father absence "the most pressing issue facing America today." Alarmed by growing evidence of the importance of fatherhood, President Barack Obama, who was raised by a single mother, has forcefully pleaded with fathers to step up throughout his presidency.

"In many ways, I came to understand the importance of fatherhood through its absence—both in my life and in the lives of others," Obama wrote in a 2009 Father's Day piece in *Parade* magazine. "I came to understand that the hole a man leaves when he abandons his responsibility to his children is one that no government can fill. We can do everything possible to provide good jobs and good schools and safe streets for our kids, but it will never be enough to fully make up the difference."

Where Did Daddy Go?

DeBoer doesn't remember much about his father. His mom and dad divorced shortly after he was born, and since then, DeBoer's only seen him twice. What he does remember is sitting alone in bed at night, covers pulled up around his chin, wondering, "Why didn't my dad want me? Am I not good enough?"

"I've spent a lot of my life hating him," DeBoer said. "It made me angry that he would abandon me like that."

The increase of father absence in America is born of several intertwining trends, said Alan Hawkins, a professor in BYU's [Brigham Young University's] School of Family Life. While the divorce rate has dropped in recent years, it's not an indication that more families are staying together. Rather, Hawkins said, more people are choosing not to get married in the first place.

For many years, marriage and children "were a packaged deal," he said, "and society was pretty good at enforcing that with strong cultural norms." Things started shifting during the sexual revolution of the '60s and '70s. Now, polls indicate, a majority of Americans are opposed to the idea of a "shotgun wedding," or getting married just because a woman is pregnant.

The move away from marriage is a result of a bigger shift in American values that Hawkins calls a loss of "child centeredness." At one time, society expected adults to make decisions based largely on what was best for the children.

"Marriage isn't about kids anymore," he said. "It's about my satisfaction as an adult, my emotional well-being, my personal development."

A large percentage of today's young moms and dads are children of divorce and, therefore, wary of marriage. For many, Hawkins said, the logical solution is cohabitation. In 1960, there were only about 197,000 unmarried couples raising children together, the U.S. Census Bureau reported. In 2009, there were more than 2.5 million.

"Most of these couples are together when the baby comes and they have high hopes for staying that way," Hawkins said. "Unfortunately, only a small percentage are able to hold that together and solidify that relationship. It's even easier to leave your kid when you haven't got a legal commitment holding you there."

In a five-year study following 5,000 children, the Brookings Institution, a nonprofit public policy organization based in Washington, D.C., found 80 percent of fathers provide support to mothers during pregnancy and more than 70 percent visit their children at the hospital. At the time of birth, a vast majority indicated they wanted to help raise their child.

Five years down the road, however, only 35 percent of unmarried couples had gotten married. About 40 percent of unmarried mothers had already broken up with their child's father and entered into at least one new partnership. Fourteen percent had a child with a new partner.

"Most fathers care about their children," said Victor Nelson, a marriage and family therapist from Logan [Utah].

"They've given up on making things work with the mother, but most want to figure out some sort of solution for their kids."

But even if fathers keep in touch after a breakup, children suffer, said Nelson, who specializes in helping couples make co-parenting plans after a relationship has gone south.

"The bottom line is, kids really need frequent contact with both parents to successfully navigate developmental stages as they grow up," he said.

Growing Up Without Dad

While he's careful to take responsibility for the way he's run his life up to this point—criminal record and all—in the back of his mind, DeBoer, who dropped out of high school to help his mother provide for his younger siblings, has always wondered if things might have been different had his father been around.

The family was poor. At times, DeBoer's mother worked three jobs in order to pay the bills.

"She worked so hard," DeBoer said. "There wasn't nothing she wouldn't do for us kids."

But the combination of a working mom who wasn't around much and living in a crime-riddled, low-income neighborhood proved difficult for DeBoer. The first time he got arrested, he was 17 years old. He started drinking in middle school. He picked up drugs in high school. When he started drifting toward gang activity, his mother sent him away to live with his aunt and uncle. DeBoer continued, though, down the path he'd started.

"My dad wasn't there to teach me how to be a man, so I looked to my friends," he said. "I didn't have no one to look up to. I had to teach myself everything."

The research backs DeBoer up.

A study by the Wisconsin Department of Health and Social Services [now Wisconsin Department of Health Services] found only 13 percent of juvenile delinquents come from families where the biological mother and father are married to each other. Thirty-three percent come from families where the parents have divorced. Forty-four percent have parents who were never married. The University of Pennsylvania and Princeton University both found young men who grow up in homes without fathers are twice as likely to end up in jail as those who come from traditional two-parent families—even when other factors like race, income, parent education and urban residence were held constant.

"Something about not having a father in the picture seems to make at least certain types of boys more likely to engage in aggressive violent behavior," said Bradford Wilcox, director of the National Marriage Project at the University of Virginia. "The theory is, they are trying to signal to others they are a man. If they don't have a good model in the household, they are more likely to embrace what they see on TV or what they see their friends doing."

Today's dads still bring the majority of financial resources to the table, Wilcox said. Money translates into things like food, tutoring and college.

Despite socioeconomic status, however, just having a father at home makes a child more likely to succeed at school, according to a study by the Charles F. Kettering Foundation. Children from low-income, two-parent families outperform students from high-income, single-parent homes. Almost twice as many high achievers come from two-parent homes as one-parent homes.

Children who grow up without a father in the home are also more likely to run away from home and commit suicide, according to the U.S. Department of Health and Human Services. Eighty-five percent of children with behavioral disorders don't have a father at home.

"Dads tend to have a stricter, more firm approach to discipline than moms," Wilcox said. "They are physically bigger. They have deeper voices. They are more likely to command attention and compliance—especially when dealing with teenage boys. Kids need that hard line to develop an appropriate sense of right and wrong."

For girls, living in a father-absent home has physical consequences. Without a father, said Erin Holmes, an assistant professor in BYU's School of Family Life, girls tend to go through puberty sooner. A recent study by three U.S. universities found the earlier a father left, the greater risk a girl was at for getting pregnant as a teen.

Fatherlessness is also associated with eating disorders and depression, Holmes said.

"It could be these girls are trying to fill an emotional void," Holmes said. "We don't know. What we do know, though, is that not having dad around can be devastating."

A Dad Who's Really There

DeBoer doesn't really refer to his father as "Dad"—he gives that title to another man who lived with his mother briefly during his elementary school years. That man, he remembers, "loved me," DeBoer said, "I know he did because he showed me. He took me to Lagoon [amusement park in Utah], to the zoo. He spent time with me."

Being a father is more than just being male and showing up, said Holmes, who studies the effects of father involvement. Children who have poor relationships with their fathers or even those whose fathers are away from home working for extensive periods of time are at risk for some of the same problems as a child without a father, she said. Children whose fathers spend a lot of time with them and build a strong emotional bond report, however, higher levels of happiness and better social adjustment than children who don't consider their relationship with their father to be particularly strong.

"Sometimes fathers aren't in homes because they weren't doing good fathering," Holmes said. "We're not just saying, 'Let's get dads back in homes.' We're saying, 'Let's get dads doing good fathering.'"

DeBoer gave up parties, smoking and beer to make sure he's there to sing little Lucius to sleep and get him breakfast in the morning. He even quit swearing after he realized his son was apt to copy him. To his father's delight, the little boy's first word was "Papa."

"I don't know how a dad cannot be a dad," he said. "It makes me so happy to be around my son. I hate leaving him when I go to work."

He's only 17 months into fatherhood, and DeBoer knows he will make mistakes. He is adamant, though, that he won't make the same one his dad made.

"I'm going to be there for him day in and day out," he said. "I want him to stay out of trouble and go to college. I'm gonna do everything in my power to make sure he has the best shot at life I can give him."

> "Not all fathers have the capacity to benefit the lives of their children with their presence, no matter how loudly and vehemently we insist they do."

Children Are Not Necessarily Damaged by the Absence of Fathers

Michele Weldon

Michele Weldon is an author, a journalist, the director of programs at Illinois Humanities Council, and an educator at Northwestern University's Medill School of Journalism. In the following viewpoint, she rejects the idea that children growing up without a father in the house will inevitably face a dismal future beset by crime, financial instability, and emotional anguish. Weldon turns to her own family, in which she is the single mother to three flourishing young men, to prove that a missing father does not doom children. She maintains that children raised by single mothers need society's support, not blame. It is essential, she argues, that the sons and daughters of fathers who have abandoned their fatherly obligations be given every chance to succeed and not told by moralists that their lives are a predetermined failure.

As you read, consider the following questions:

1. According to Weldon, how many American children are being raised without a father?

2. What fictional fathers does Weldon point to as examples of exemplary role models?

3. What are the goals of President Barack Obama's fatherhood initiative, according to the author?

My middle son, Brendan, graduated from the Ohio State University [OSU] last month [in May 2013] with an undergraduate degree in four years. He was the only one of his close high school friends not on the five- or six-year plan, the only one of his roommates in the house on Chittenden Street to earn a diploma on time.

I drove from Chicago to Columbus in my sister's blue Toyota van with the seats removed and 130,000 miles on the odometer to be in the Horseshoe stadium all Buckeyes call The Shoe. I screeched as he received his diploma along with more than 10,000 other sons and daughters in caps and gowns who listened as President Barack Obama implored the graduates to "dare to dream bigger."

A Missing Father

The next morning, we loaded the van with Brendan's clothes, books, desk and anything else worth keeping, leaving behind an old mattress and a black pleather chair minus a wheel. Brendan's father missed his graduation. He also missed Brendan's high school and eighth-grade graduations, plus nearly a decade of birthdays and holidays, Brendan's knee surgery, the day he received his driver's license, his first love and four moves into college dorms and apartments, plus four moves back home.

Likewise, my sons' father missed my oldest son, Weldon's, graduation from high school, his graduation from the University of Wisconsin in 2011 and this summer, he will miss his graduation from a master's program in contemporary history at Universidad de Compultense in Madrid. He also missed my youngest son, Colin's, eighth-grade graduation in 2008 and high school graduation last year. I have no reason to believe he will be present for Colin's expected graduation from the University of Iowa in 2016.

Their father has had only a handful of contacts—a few letters, one or two phone calls, a session I arranged with a family therapist—with his children for nearly a decade. My boys and I have lived in the same house for 18 years with the same landline. I have had the same job with the same office phone for 17 years; the same email addresses for the last 17 years as well.

Their father has not passed, nor is he incarcerated, incapacitated or otherwise separated from his sons against his will. I do not know for sure where he lives or what he does—even on what continent. I know from court documents he claims zero income on his tax forms and alternately lists three different addresses. Their father, an able-bodied, former litigating attorney who was the editor of law review at a top law school, has chosen absence from his sons' lives—physically, emotionally, financially, spiritually, virtually.

A Thriving Family

While so many people may cluck their tongues in pity and bemoan the father hunger my sons must feel, I emphatically defy the claim that all fatherless children need pity; my sons are thriving.

There is another story we must tell in this complicated scenario: the positive one where a father who abandons his children does not have the power to annihilate their futures.

Their father and I have been divorced since 1996; he moved to Amsterdam in 2004 with two weeks' notice and a declining interest in anything related to them. Shortly after his move, he stopped paying support and eventually stopped calling, writing or ever showing up for anything.

This story is far from unique. 24 million children in this country live in homes without a father. And these children need our support as a society, not our finger-wagging blame.

My three sons (now 19, 22 and 24) have not interacted meaningfully with their father in nine years, save the brief chatter he muttered to them when we arrived at his own father's funeral on January 12, 2008. It was the day after both Brendan and Colin's birthdays—when Brendan had turned 17 and Colin turned 14. It was another pair of same-day birthdays their father did not acknowledge.

An Epic Legal Battle

But he has contacted me through the courts—with a rigorous campaign to prove he should not have to pay any past, present or future court-ordered support. In December of 2012, after years of his filings and my responses, and five years after he filed for bankruptcy (coincidentally, the same year our oldest started college), I settled in court for less than 10 percent of what he owed for his sons. Their father handed my attorney a cashier's check for an amount that was less than one year's out-of-state tuition at OSU. It was better than nothing, and I needed it.

As another Father's Day approaches this coming Sunday, the commercialized tributes to the romantic ideal of loving, present and omniscient fathers punctuate the media along with the cultural conviction that the flip side—childhood without a father, any father—is a life lost.

Rejecting the Rhetoric

While I joyously support the necessary push to elevate the role of fathers, I insist that the rhetoric from studies and pundits should not be that a fatherless life is always worse for the children. My sons reap the effects of support from my brothers and sisters, extended family, an amazing high school wrestling coach, teachers and mentors who love them. And, of course, from me.

Certainly, it is optimal to have two parents if at all possible who love and nurture their children. Certainly, some mothers present deleterious and sometimes dangerous influences on their families. Certainly, many fathers are great men who fulfill their roles admirably—they are fictional fathers like Atticus Finch in *To Kill a Mockingbird* or real-life fathers like Chris Gardner portrayed in *Pursuit of Happyness*.

But real life is not the movies.

President Obama's $1.5 billion fatherhood initiative [National Responsible Fatherhood Clearinghouse] drives home the noble intention to transform men who father children into active, involved parents and to support men to be better fathers. But in some cases, no amount of money will transform a man into a dad.

A Radical Movement

The proponents of the fathers' rights movement respond to any such refutation with vitriol and venom; they place blame on mothers' antagonism and a judicial system and culture that belittles paternal involvement. I know, I have received the trolling threats, the most recent to an opinion piece I wrote in the *New York Times* from an anonymous blogger with an inscrutable name with the headline, "F--- You, Michele Weldon."

He writes:

> She says it because every single year when the day approaches, the single day of the year that we are supposed to show fathers our love and admiration, pieces of shit like Michele Weldon feel the need to write negative pieces about fathers, no opportunity to demonize them can pass by for feminist ideologues like Ms. Weldon. . . . What we don't need is feminist ideologues in universities poisoning the minds of the future of our society to consider fathers as unneeded and unnecessary. F--- You, Michele Weldon.

Social Welfare Programs

Social welfare, in its modern sense, refers to policies and programs, typically initiated or administered by government or public bodies, intended to ameliorate social problems and improve the well-being of individuals and families with recognized needs. These needs include health care for the sick, nourishment for the hungry, and the provisions of life for the elderly, the disabled, and the poor. In traditional societies, past and present, responsibility for the welfare of individuals would be assumed collectively by their kin, either through extended family or clan structures, or by churches. Modern societies in the developed world have created different models for state involvement in social welfare, with variations reflecting each nation's cultural values and level of available public resources.

"Social Welfare Programs,"
Global Issues in Context Online Collection, 2015.

But this is not about me. This is about the men I raise who will one day be good fathers—better than the one they knew.

My sons have lived a different existence; one where their father chose himself over them, every day for years, and continues to do so. He deliberately elected to disappear from their lives—incrementally at first, fading from their days, weeks and months like a Polaroid kept in a drawer—then completely.

A Predetermined Future?

I try to be reassuring, to say their father is intelligent, athletic, handsome—all traits of his they inherited. I say fatherless men can succeed. Sometimes, I feel as if I am just mouthing words that make no sound as they leave my lips, that they are mere abstract distractions of syllables—sparks of smoke in the face of such gaping wounds. I understand the void left by a parent's abandonment is vacuous and painful. I cannot fix this, I cannot make their father be someone he is not. I have never been able to fix it, make up for it. But I will never agree that because they are fatherless they are marked for lives marred by mistakes with drugs, alcohol, delinquency and crime.

They are not less-than, they have no predetermined failure; they have proven otherwise.

Nothing stays broken forever if you don't want it to—not a life, not a career, not a relationship, not a body, not a family, not a home, not a heart. You can choose to leave behind the pain, the judgment, the hurt, and escape from the events that led to this aftermath, and be someone who finds the love he needs to move forward. Some researchers agree with me; you can fill the black hole left by someone else's choice.

A Reminder

My father's gold medal hangs on a heavy chain that falls to the middle of my chest. On one side of the cracker-sized disc is an image of Mary holding Jesus as an infant. She has a halo—a crown really—and the medal is framed in elaborate filigree. On the other side in capital letters is engraved: "WM G WELDON," and underneath his name is his 9-digit social security number.

It is the medal he wore every day as a private first class in the U.S. Army during World War II. He told me once he is sure this talisman is what kept him alive. When my father died in January 1988, my mother, two brothers and three sisters and I carefully sorted through all his watches and cufflinks, hats and books. From that bounty, among other treasures, my sisters entrusted his medal to me.

By the time my father died, none of my three boys were yet born; Weldon arrived in October of that year. They did not know Papa Bill, though many remark that Brendan resembles him—with his oval, handsome face, bright blue eyes and dimpled chin. Each one of the boys has his kindness.

I felt unconditionally loved by both my parents every day of my life. My boys will never know that feeling, and that arouses grief and regret in my choice of a man who eventually left them. But without him, these magnificent sons would not exist and the world would be less than it is.

I have come to realize that not all men are like my father, and that not all men are good fathers in spite of the Subaru commercials and clips from *Modern Family*. Not all fathers have the capacity to benefit the lives of their children with their presence, no matter how loudly and vehemently we insist they do.

We have no business shaming the sons and daughters of fathers who neglect their innate and moral responsibilities. For Father's Day and every day, let us remember we owe it to all children who have suffered paternal absence to convince them they can always and forever overcome the sins of the fathers.

Periodical and Internet Sources Bibliography

The following articles have been selected to supplement the diverse views presented in this chapter.

Emily Badger

"The Unbelievable Rise of Single Motherhood in America over the Last 50 Years," *Washington Post*, December 18, 2014.

Noah Berlatsky

"What the Rising Number of Single Dads Says About Fatherhood in General," *Atlantic*, July 3, 2013.

Katy Chatel

"I'm a Single Mother by Choice. One Parent Can Be Better than Two," *Washington Post*, March 16, 2015.

Caroline Davey

"Making It Work as a Single Dad," *Modern Fatherhood*, June 15, 2013.

Helen Davidson

"Half of Working Mothers Face Discrimination at Work, Study Finds," *Guardian*, July 24, 2014.

Gail Gross

"The Important Role of Dad," *Huffington Post*, June 12, 2014.

Gretchen Livingston

"The Rise of Single Fathers," Pew Research Center, July 2, 2013.

Christine Mungai

"Children 'Better Off' with Single Mothers in Poor Nations, Report Suggests," *Mail & Guardian Africa*, July 13, 2014.

Reihan Salam

"The Uneven Impact of Single Parenting on Women and Men," *National Review Online*, March 20, 2013.

Ariane Sherine

"Being a Single Parent Is No Picnic," *Guardian*, January 4, 2014.

Valerie Young

"Single Mothers, Double Standard," Moms Rising.org, April 30, 2013.

How Should the Government Treat Single-Parent Families?

Chapter Preface

In 2003 the administration of US President George W. Bush launched the Healthy Marriage Initiative (HMI), a series of programs funded by the US Department of Health and Human Services' Administration for Children and Families (ACF) to strengthen marriages and teach marriage skills to young men and women in primarily low-income communities all over the country. The programs would be administered by private contractors with proven track records and would be voluntary for all participants.

Wade Horn, the assistant secretary for Children and Families, outlined what the program was not about in his 2002 testimony before the US Senate Committee on Finance. It would not, he asserted, be concerned with forcing people to marry or stay in abusive relationships, nor would government officials be authorized to threaten to cut off government benefits to single-parent families if they did not take part. Instead, such programs would remove any disincentives to marry, teach valuable marriage and parenting skills, and provide mentorship for young couples with children. In his testimony, he deemed a well-funded and vibrant healthy marriage initiative as central to his department's efforts to keep families out of poverty and communities productive and safe.

From 2001 to 2014, the US Congress allocated nearly $800 million to the HMI. The HMI was controversial from the very start. Although the idea that marriage is a social good that benefits families and communities had been central to public policy for many years, the idea that government should allocate hundreds of millions of dollars to foster strong marriages and teach men and women how to be in healthy relationships generated criticism from many on the different sides of the political spectrum.

Fiscal conservatives began to question the value of such programs, particularly when the American economy went into a nosedive in 2008. For many on the left, the government was promoting stereotypes of single mothers and single-parent families and bribing men and women to marry. For many policy makers, marriage programs were not a cost-effective way to approach the problems of poverty, income inequality, and divorce. In addition, many critics of the HMI argued that the government should stay out of the marriage-promotion business.

By 2010 critics of the program were pointing to statistics that showed that the national marriage rate continued to decline while the government poured money into marriage-promotion programs as proof that the HMI was not effective. One analysis, conducted by the Council on Contemporary Families, found that marriage did not provide help for low-income, unmarried mothers that Bush administration officials predicted. It also found evidence that marriage-promotion programs had no effect on whether couples stayed together or got married. For the fathers who took part in the HMI, there was no evidence that they spent more time with or financially supported their children than fathers who did not participate.

As the council's report concluded, "If the goal of marriage promotion efforts was truly to lower poverty rates and improve the well-being of unmarried parents and their children, then it is time to take a different approach toward this goal." The report recommended instead that government programs should address the issue of unintended pregnancy in order to provide meaningful help to young single parents in low-income communities.

The role of the government in promoting marriage is one of the subjects explored in the following chapter, which focuses on how the government should treat single-parent families. Other viewpoints in the chapter consider the impact of federal welfare programs on marriage rates and the need to address economic inequalities outside of marriage.

| "So while many women are working
hard to support themselves and their
families, they're still facing unfair
choices, outdated workplace policies."

Stronger Federal Economic and Social Policies Would Help Single-Parent Families

Barack Obama

Barack Obama is the forty-fourth president of the United States. In the following viewpoint, he proposes several economic and social policies that would ensure that women are full and equal participants in the US economy. Although this effort is important to him because he was raised by a single mother, he points out that it is necessary to provide full opportunities for women for the country's economic health. He lists several policies that would help single mothers, including raising the minimum wage, paid family leave, subsidized day care, and equal pay for equal work. Obama cites the Patient Protection and Affordable Care Act (PPACA, also known as Obamacare) as one policy that is already helping women by providing affordable health care. Obama concludes that when American women succeed, the country also succeeds.

Barack Obama, "Remarks by the President on Women and the Economy," October 31, 2014. WhiteHouse.gov. Courtesy of whitehouse.gov.

131

As you read, consider the following questions:

1. According to Obama, what percentage of the Rhode Island College student body are women?

2. What does Obama identify as the average age of workers who would benefit from an increase in the minimum wage?

3. What Rhode Island company does the president praise as being proactive in recruiting talented young women?

Now, the good news is we've made a lot of progress since the worst economic crisis of our lifetimes. So when I first came into office, the economy was in a freefall, the auto industry was in a freefall. Banks were frozen up. We were losing 800,000 jobs a month. Over the past 55 months, our businesses have now added 10.3 million new jobs. For the first time in more than six years, the unemployment rate is below 6 percent. Over the past six months, our economy has grown at its fastest pace in more than 10 years.

And in education, dropout rates are down, the national graduation rate is the highest on record, more young people are earning their college degrees than ever before. Good job, young people.

In energy, we're less dependent on foreign oil than any time in nearly three decades. Manufacturing—the quintessential producer of middle-class jobs, the heart of Rhode Island's economy for decades—manufacturing has now created 700,000 new jobs since early 2010. Ten million Americans have gained the peace of mind that comes with having health insurance.

AUDIENCE MEMBER: Thank you!

THE PRESIDENT: You're welcome.

Deficits have come down. Health care inflation has come down. There's almost no economic measure by which we haven't made substantial progress over this period of time. We're better off than we were.

Steady Progress

So, look, the progress has been hard. It's sometimes been challenging in particular states. But it's been steady and it's been real. Now, the thing is, though, what's also true is that millions of Americans don't yet feel the benefits of a growing economy where it matters most—and that's in their own lives. There are still a lot of folks who are working hard, but having trouble making ends meet.

I know that many of you are working while you go to school. Some of you are helping support your parents or siblings. Here in Rhode Island, and across the country, there are still too many people who are working too many hours and don't have enough to show for it. And this isn't just the hangover from the Great Recession; some of this has to do with trends that date back 20, 30 years. And I've always said that recovering from the crisis of 2008 was the first thing we had to do, but our economy won't be healthy until we reverse some of these longer-term trends, this erosion of middle-class jobs and income.

And here in Rhode Island, my administration recently announced a grant to help more long-term unemployed folks get the training and mentoring they need to get back to work. And all across the country, we're taking similar actions, community by community, to keep making progress.

We've got to harness the momentum that we're seeing in the broader economy and make sure the economy is working for every single American. We've got to keep making smart choices. And today, here at RIC [Rhode Island College], I want to focus on some commonsense steps we can take to help working families right now. In particular, I want to zero in on the choices we need to make to ensure that women are full and equal participants in the economy.

Focusing on Women

Now, men, I don't want you to feel neglected. . . . But part of the reason that I want this focus is because I was raised by a single mom, and know what it was like for her to raise two kids and go to work at the same time, and try to piece things together without a lot of support. And my grandmother, who never graduated from college but worked her way up to become vice president of a bank, I know what it was like for her to hit the glass ceiling, and to see herself passed over for promotions by people that she had trained. And so some of this is personal, but some of it is also what we know about our economy, which is it's changing in profound ways, and in many ways for the better because of the participation of women more fully in our economy.

So earlier today, I met with a group of women business owners and working moms . . . and they were sharing stories that probably sound familiar to a lot of people—studying for finals after working a full shift; searching for child care when the babysitter cancels at the last minute; using every penny of their savings so they can afford to stay home with their new baby.

And so I kept on hearing my own story. I kept on hearing about my mom struggling to put herself through school, or my grandmother hitting that glass ceiling. And I thought about Michelle, and I told some stories about when Michelle and I were younger and getting started, and we were struggling to balance two careers while raising a family. And my job forced me to travel a lot, which made it harder on Michelle, and we would feel some of the guilt that so many people feel—we're working, we're thinking about the kids, we're wondering whether we're bad parents, we're wondering whether we were doing what we need to do on the job. And as the catch-22 of working parents, we wanted to spend time with our kids, but we also wanted to make sure that we gave them the opportunities that our hard work was providing.

And then, of course, I think about my daughters. And the idea that my daughters wouldn't have the same opportunities as somebody's sons—well, that's unacceptable. That's not acceptable.

So I say all this because—to the men here, we all have a stake in choosing policies that help women succeed. Women make up about half of America's workforce. For more than two decades, women have earned over half of the higher education degrees awarded in this country. And you look at the RIC student body, almost 70 percent women. In colleges nationwide, there are more women graduating than men—which means that for the first time, America's highly educated workforce will be made up of more women than men.

Women Deserve Better

But here's the challenge—that's all good news—the challenge is, our economy and some of the laws and rules governing our workplaces haven't caught up with that reality. A lot of workplaces haven't caught up with that reality. So while many women are working hard to support themselves and their families, they're still facing unfair choices, outdated workplace policies. That holds them back, but it also holds all of us back. We have to do better, because women deserve better. And, by the way, when women do well, everybody does well.

So women deserve a day off to care for a sick child or sick parent without running into hardship. And Rhode Island has got the right idea. You're one of just three states where paid family leave is the law of the land. More states should choose to follow your lead.

It was interesting talking to some of the small business owners in the meeting. They were saying how the Rhode Island law actually helped them do a better job recruiting and retaining outstanding employees. And so that shows you something—that this is not just a nice thing to do; it's good policy. It's good for business. It's good for the economy.

Sound Economic Policies

Without paid leave, when a baby arrives or an aging parent needs help, workers have to make painful decisions about whether they can afford to be there when their families need them most. Many women can't even get a paid day off to give birth to their child. I mean, there are a lot of companies that still don't provide maternity leave. Of course, dads should be there, too. So let's make this happen for women and for men, and make our economy stronger. We've got to broaden our laws for family leave.

Moms and dads deserve a great place to drop their kids off every day that doesn't cost them an arm and a leg. We need better child care, day care, early childhood education policies. In many states, sending your child to day care costs more than sending them to a public university.

AUDIENCE MEMBER: True!

THE PRESIDENT: True. And too often, parents have no choice but to put their kids in cheaper day care that maybe doesn't have the kinds of programming that makes a big difference in a child's development. And sometimes there may just not be any slots, or the best programs may be too far away. And sometimes, someone, usually mom, leaves the workplace to stay home with the kids, which then leaves her earning a lower wage for the rest of her life as a result. And that's not a choice we want Americans to make.

So let's make this happen. By the end of this decade, let's enroll 6 million children in high-quality preschool, and let's make sure that we are making America stronger. That is good for families; it's also good for the children, because we know investing in high-quality early childhood education makes all the difference in the world, and those kids will do better. So we need family leave, we need better child care policies, and we need to make sure that women get an honest day's pay for an honest day's work.

About 28 million Americans would benefit if we raised the minimum wage to $10.10 an hour—like [Rhode Island politicians] Sheldon Whitehouse and Jack Reed support. And let me say this: Minimum wage—those aren't just teenage jobs that are impacted. We're not just talking about young people. My first job was at Baskin-Robbins. And I got paid the minimum wage and it was okay. Wearing that hat and the apron was—(laughter)—yeah.

But the truth is, the average worker who would benefit from an increase in the minimum wage is 35 years old—35. A majority of low-wage workers are women. A lot of them have kids. Right now, somebody working full-time on the minimum wage makes $14,500 a year—$14,500. If they're a parent, that means they're below the poverty line. Nobody who works full-time in America should be below the poverty line. They should not be raising their kids below the poverty line. I am not going to give up this fight. And we need Republicans in Congress to stop blocking a minimum wage increase and give America a raise.

And if a woman is doing the same work as a man, she deserves to get paid just like the man does. Even though it's 2014, there are women still earning less than men for doing the same work. And women of color face an even greater wage gap. And at a time when women are the primary breadwinners in more households than ever, that hurts the whole family if they're not getting paid fairly. Again, men, I just want you to pay attention. When Michelle and I were starting off, there were stretches of time where Michelle was making more money than me, and I wanted to make sure she was making every dime that she deserved. Right? I don't know how I benefit by her getting paid less than a man. Right?

AUDIENCE: Right!

THE PRESIDENT: Okay! Men, I just want you to be clear.

And it starts with recent college graduates. Women often start their careers with lower pay, and then the gap grows over

time—especially if they get passed over for promotions and then they get fewer raises, or they take time off to care for family members. So you get a situation where women are doing the same work as men, but the structure, the expectations somehow is, well, they'll take time off for family, and once they take time off that means that it's okay to pay them a little bit less. And that builds up over time.

Embracing the 21st Century

And we've got to have a reversal of those kinds of policies and that kind of mind-set. We've got to catch up to the 21st century. We need to pass a fair pay law, make our economy stronger. It will be good for America, and it will be good for our families and good for our kids.

While we're on the topic, women deserve to make their own health care choices—not politicians or insurance companies. And that's why the Affordable Care Act [referring to the Patient Protection and Affordable Care Act, commonly known as Obamacare] is so important. Insurance plans—because we passed the Affordable Care Act, insurance plans now have to cover the basics, including contraceptive care, and prenatal care, and maternity care.

That means a working mom doesn't have to put off the care she needs just so she can pay her bills on time. Tens of millions of women have new access to preventive care like mammograms with no co-pays, no out-of-pocket expenses. It means that a cash-strapped student doesn't have to choose between the care that she needs and the cost of textbooks.

And because of the Affordable Care Act, because of Obamacare—(applause)—because of that law, no insurance company can deny you coverage based on a preexisting condition like breast cancer, or charge you more for the same care just because you're a woman. That's the right thing to do.

So no matter how many times Republicans threaten to repeal this law, we're going to keep it in place—because it's working. Not only is it covering more people, not only is it protecting women and people with preexisting conditions from discrimination, but it's actually been part of the trend that's lowering health care inflation. We're actually saving money because the system is getting smarter and there's more preventive care instead of emergency care, and we're changing how health care is delivered. Which is why I'm pretty sure that in 10 years they're not going to call it Obamacare anymore. Republicans will be like, oh, I was for that, yes. That's how that works.

AUDIENCE MEMBER: We'll remember.

THE PRESIDENT: You'll remember though. You'll remind them.

Now, to really make sure that women are full and equal participants in our economy, we can do some of this administratively. But it requires not just changing laws; it requires changing attitudes. And more and more companies are changing attitudes. And this is really good news.

The Role of Business

JetBlue, for example, has a flexible work-from-home plan for its customer service reps. They've found it's led to happier, more productive employees and lower costs. Google increased paid leave for new parents—moms and dads—to five months—five months—and that helped cut the rate of women leaving the company by half. And when I was having a conversation with some of the women business owners before I came out here, they were saying it's really costly when you lose a good employee and you've got to train somebody all over again. It's much more sensible from a business perspective to invest in them and make them feel like you've got their backs, and they'll stay with you.

And it's not just these big corporations that are embracing these policies. So Cheryl Snead, who is the CEO [chief executive officer] of Banneker Industries—where's Cheryl? She was here just a second. There she is back there. So Banneker Industries, a supply chain management firm, is based in North Smithfield. And when Cheryl was in college, she studied mechanical engineering. At the time, there weren't that many African American women in mechanical engineering. There still aren't. We're working to change that.

Cheryl wants to do something about that. Her company has made it a priority to find talented young women and minority students, encourage them to study science and math in college, hire them once they graduate. And what Cheryl was explaining was that having a diverse workforce, having more women in the workforce, all that makes her a stronger company. And it's not just good for the workers—it's good for business.

So if large businesses like Google, small businesses like Cheryl's all see the wisdom of this, let's join them. Let's encourage more women and more girls into fields like science and technology and engineering and math. And let's work with those companies to ensure that family-friendly policies can support more women in that workforce.

Ann-Marie Harrington—where is Ann? Ann-Marie is right here. So Ann-Marie, she's the president of a company called Embolden, based in Pawtucket. And it provides web services to community foundations and nonprofits. A small business—about 20 employees; 21 I think she said. She just hired somebody, must have been. But she lets them work from home and keep a flexible schedule when they need to. And she says that's increased her company's productivity.

Federal Policies

So I'm taking a page from these companies' playbooks. This summer I directed the federal agencies in the executive branch to put flexible workplace policies in wherever possible; make it clear that all federal employees have the right to request them. We want the best talent to serve our country, and that means making it a little bit easier for them to maintain that work-family balance.

But these are issues that are too important to hinge on whether or not your boss is enlightened. We have to raise our voices to demand that women get paid fairly. We've got to raise our voices to make sure women can take time off to care for a loved one, and that moms and dads can spend time with a new baby. We've got to raise our voices to make sure that our women maintain and keep their own health care choices. We've got to raise our voices to basically do away with policies and politicians that belong in a *Mad Men* episode. *Mad Men* is a good show, but that's not who we want making decisions about our workplaces these days. When women succeed, America succeeds. And we need leaders who understand that. That's what we need.

So if you care about these policies, you got to keep pushing for them. This shouldn't be partisan. Republicans and Democrats should be supportive of all these issues.

I was talking to Tom Perez [the US secretary of labor]; he had just come back from Europe. He was talking to chambers of commerce and conservative politicians. They were all supportive of family leave, supportive of child care, because they understood it actually made the economy more productive. This isn't a liberal or conservative agenda.

When I talk to women, like the ones I spoke to earlier, when I hear folks' stories from across the country, and when I think about my own mom and how she made it all work, or my grandmother, nobody is looking at these issues through partisan lenses. We're not Democrats first or Republicans first, we are Americans first. And as Americans, it's up to us to protect and restore the ideals that made this country great.

And that is, that in this country, no matter who you are, what you look like, where you come from, whether you are male or you are female—here in America, you can make it if you try. That's the promise of America. That's the future I'm going to fight for. I want you to fight there with me.

> "When we work here [in the US Congress], we try to do the right thing, on both sides of the aisle, but we never know, for sometimes decades, whether we did more good than damage."

Federal Policies Discourage Marriage and Perpetuate Government Dependence

Louie Gohmert

Louie Gohmert is a US congressman from Texas. In the following viewpoint, he applauds the US Congress's efforts in separating food stamps from the agricultural bill, a move that he hopes will allow a serious debate on the food stamp program and lead to much-needed reform. Gohmert asserts that the food stamp program, like other types of public assistance programs, perpetuates government dependence and stifles economic achievement. He recalls his time as a federal judge, where he saw numerous young, single mothers come before his court looking for a handout instead of going out and finding a job. Although well intentioned, he says, government assistance functions to discourage these women from marriage, encourages them to have more children on taxpayers' money, and prevents them from living up to

Louie Gohmert, "Dependence on the Government," July 11, 2013. Congress.gov. Courtesy of Congress.gov.

their full potential. Therefore, he argues, there needs to be a thorough reassessment of these programs to eliminate waste, fraud, and abuse.

As you read, consider the following questions:

1. What does Gohmert identify as Adam's job in the Garden of Eden?

2. In what year did Newt Gingrich put forth the Contract with America, according to the viewpoint?

3. According to Gohmert, what percentage of the farm program was made up of the food stamp program?

Today, despite all of the diatribe, all of the allegations, so many of which shocked me, this bill passed [the Agricultural Act of 2014]. There were things in the farm bill I was not crazy about, but what an extraordinary day for this reason: Over the last 40–50 years, members of the other party [referring to Democrats] have increasingly made the United States a welfare state where more and more American people are dependent upon this government for their livelihood. Having been at a Harvard [University] orientation course, I was shocked to have a dean there with charts that showed that since welfare began, and assistance to single moms, a check actually for each child that any woman could have out of wedlock, they would get a check from the government. Now, it was well-intentioned.

Back in the sixties, there were deadbeat dads that were not helping with their obligation to help their children, and so the government, people here in Congress thought, wow, why don't we help these poor single moms by giving them a check for every child they have out of wedlock. At that time we were around 6–7 percent of children being born to single-parent homes. And after 40 years—actually after 30 years, as economists will tell you, you will get more of what you pay for. And so we are to date now past 40 percent and moving toward 50 percent of children born in America to a single-mom home because we got what we paid for.

A Luring Offer

Now, it doesn't matter how well-intentioned the program was. What I saw happening in the nineties as a judge was single moms coming before me for welfare fraud, and the stories were usually the same that they presented to me. So often they were bored with high school, and someone said, hey, you can just have a baby and the government will send you a check. And then you can live, and you don't have to work. You don't have to finish high school.

And those well-intentioned members of Congress back in the sixties ended up in effect luring smart young women away from finishing high school into having a child out of wedlock and away from reaching their full potential.

Now, even for those of us who are Christians that believe God created Heaven and Earth, and that God created at one time a Garden of Eden from which man fell for disobedience, even in that scenario when the world was perfect, Adam was given a job. In a perfect world where everything was fantastic—before childbirth pains, before briars, before thistles, before all of the things that frustrate farmers, at that time he had a job: tend the garden.

In a perfect world, people will have a job to reach their God-given potential, and there is a good feeling from doing a good job in what we do.

That's one of the things I miss about working in the yard or working out on a farm or working with your hands. When you finish, you see you've done something good.

When we work here, we try to do the right thing, on both sides of the aisle, but we never know, for sometimes decades, whether we did more good than damage.

And I would humbly submit that the program that began to lure young women away from their potential, away from finishing high school, away from time in college, was well intentioned, but this government should never be in the business of luring people away from their potential, from luring people into results from which they cannot seem to extricate themselves.

And they'd come before me for welfare fraud, felony welfare fraud, as a district judge. And normally the scenario was that they realized, after a number of children, they couldn't live on that little bit of government subsistence; and they would think, well, maybe if I get a job, and I don't report it to the federal authorities, maybe I'll finally have enough income that, combined with what the government's giving me, then I can get ahead and I can get out of this hole, this rut.

The Role of Welfare Reform

And so when the Republicans took the majority, in 1995, one of the things that they wanted to do was welfare reform. And I was at that Harvard orientation seminar and was surprised when they brought out the big poster graph of single mothers' income over the 30 or so years since that program had first begun.

Single moms' income, when adjusted for inflation over that 30-year period, was flatlined. All those years, the average single mom never got ahead. She was flatlined because she was lured into that government program.

I'm not sure what the right thing was, but I think it's time to have the debate about it.

So I know that those people that passed the bills in the sixties, they had the best of intentions, but those poor single moms were flatlined for about 30 years of what they were bringing home. That's tragic. I know both sides of the aisle would want them to do better and do well and every year to do a little better. I know that feeling is on both sides of the aisle, but we disagree with how you get there.

But what really shocked me today, and I've got to say, in some cases broke my heart, is to hear friends talk about how Republicans wanted to take food out of the mouths of children. I would never insinuate or say such a motive on the part of friends across the aisle, even though I believe that that welfare program, back from the sixties, did exactly that.

I would never ascribe that motivation to friends across the aisle because I know that's not their heart. They really do want to help. They just went about it in the wrong way in the sixties.

The Contract with America

And so, in 1995, when Newt Gingrich led the Republican revolution, had the Contract with America, they put in a requirement for work. If you could work, you had to work. And it pushed people who had been subsisting on welfare, barely getting by, it pushed them into the workforce.

And this graph, about 9 years later, showed that single moms' income, when adjusted for inflation, after welfare reform, had single moms making more money. Every year that graph showed their income went up. And surely that is what both sides of the aisle would want.

And when we took up this farm bill today, I voted against it for the first vote, previously. But if we are ever going to get down to truly reforming what has become a welfare state that lures far too many people away from the job they could be doing, and from the good feeling of actually accomplishing something, and the good feeling of knowing you're reaching closer, ever closer to your potential. I was willing to vote for this today because we were going to take the food stamp program out of the agriculture bill.

And I don't know what the Senate's going to do, and I can't help what they're going to do. But I know this: Today, we had a first step in the right direction. And I agreed with my leadership, if you will separate out the food stamp program so that we can have a separate debate on the food stamp program, and even though I don't agree with a number of things in the farm bill we voted on, that was such a big deal, a tremendous stride forward.

Assessing the Food Stamp Program

People said neither the House nor the Senate would ever, ever separate the food stamp program from the [agriculture] bill because in either the House or the Senate, you had to have them tied together to get enough people from both sides, or either side to vote for the bill because you'd never get enough Republicans by themselves, you'd never get enough Democrats by themselves and you'd never get enough together unless you put the food stamp program with the farm program.

But by doing so, it prevented us from looking closely at the farm program because the food stamp program made 70 to 80 percent of the budget; and you couldn't look effectively enough at the food stamp program because it was linked with the farm program.

This was a big step, and I know there are a number of groups that I thank God for that are doing a great job. And I have friends in these groups and they've said this was a major mistake today. And I would submit, very humbly, hide and watch. This was a first major step.

The Trouble with Reform

And my goal, and I hope I live to see it, and I hope this country's around long enough that we can do it, is to take every form of public assistance, every form of public assistance, and put it into one bill, in one subcommittee of the Appropriations Committee, and they deal with all welfare, all types of public assistance. And once that happens, we can have major reform.

But the reason we have trouble having reform of this evergrowing, ever-bloated welfare state is because the public assis-

US Congressman Louie Gohmert

Serving his sixth term in the United States House of Representatives, Congressman Louie Gohmert was first sworn in January 4, 2005. He proudly represents the First District of Texas which encompasses over 12 counties stretching nearly 120 miles down the state's eastern border.

A favorite among Tea Party groups, Louie speaks often as a fellow Tea Party advocate across Texas and the United States. He boldly stands on America's founding principles and is constantly coming up with big, innovative ideas solidly based on constitutional fundamentals.

Louie serves on numerous House committees and subcommittees. Congressman Gohmert is the chairman of the Natural Resources Subcommittee on Oversight and Investigations and the vice chair of the Judiciary Subcommittee on Crime, Terrorism, Homeland Security[, and Investigations].

Prior to being elected to serve in Congress, Louie was elected to three terms as district judge in Smith County, Texas. During his tenure on the bench, he gained national and international attention for some of his innovative rulings. He was later appointed by Texas governor Rick Perry to complete a term as chief justice of the 12th Court of Appeals.

Louie received his undergraduate degree from Texas A&M University and later graduated from Baylor [University] School of Law. He is also a veteran having served his country as captain in the U.S. Army.

"Biography,"
US Congressman Louie Gohmert, 2015.

tance programs are found throughout all the committees' budgets, throughout all the appropriations. So if over here in the farm program you say, wait a minute; we need to reform the food stamp program. They go, oh, you hate children. You want to starve children, you want to starve mothers or veterans or military. You must hate all these people.

Why?

Because they're willing to say things that are not right to come in here and say. And that's what broke my heart today over and over, hearing people that surely know I would never want to take food out of the mouth of someone who could not provide for themselves. I don't know any Republican who has ever said that or would ever want that.

We want to help people who truly cannot help themselves.

And my friend across the aisle, Mr. [Jim] McDermott, at Rules [the Rules Committee], when I made a proposed amendment to separate the food stamp program from the farm bill, he said, so do you want to completely eliminate the food stamp program?

And I pointed out, no, I did not. Of course, that didn't stop the mainstream press or the left-wing blogs from spouting lies. They're accustomed to that. And God bless them, they have the freedom to do that, and they should be able to do that without this administration grabbing up all their phone records.

Eliminating Waste, Fraud, and Abuse

But it was not true, and I pointed out to Mr. McDermott what was true. No, I don't want to end it. I want to separate it out. And one day I want to have all of the public assistance in one committee, where we can see all of the ones that are redundant, those that duplicate services already provided, those where the most waste, fraud and abuse is taking place, because the thing we know, we're over $50,000 for every child of debt before they ever even have a chance to start making a living.

And we have done that, and it is immoral what we have done to future generations, loading them up with debt, just because we can't get to the bottom of waste, fraud and abuse, get to the bottom of what helps this country more than hurts it. And there will be a price today to pay someday for our negligence.

But it's not too late. We can still fix it. But a start happened today. This was a big deal, to separate the food stamp program out so we can look at it.

A Troubling Example

And a good example of what I'm talking about, how these different types of assistance are spread out through so many different budgets, was pointed out by my good friend, Dan Webster from Florida, first Republican Speaker of the [Florida] House [of Representatives], as I understand it ... was reluctant to run, did run, is elected here.

He decided to get to the bottom, just one little tiny aspect of this federal, bloated bureaucracy. How many federal programs are there that are responsible for getting people to appointments?

So far he says he's found 87 programs responsible for getting people to appointments, and most of them are in the same cities, and most of them have the vans that are the same size, same kind of vans. And on average, when they do take somebody, they'll maybe average three people per trip.

Well, when you take up one committee's budget, or one appropriations, and you were to take one of those 87 programs and say, you know what, let's combine this with these other programs, then we will hear, as we've heard today, oh, you hate children, or you want to take food from people's mouths.

If it's all 87 programs in one bill, then we can come before this body and say, no, we love children. We want to help this country. In fact, we will do more good for children of the future than what you've proposed because you're loading them up with debt, while we lavish it on our generation, and going to make future generations pay for lavishing ourselves. That is just wrong.

> *"Government reforms that promote or remove impediments to education, to work, marriage and two-parent homes would help change the direction of our country."*

The Government Should Be Promoting Marriage

Marco Rubio

Marco Rubio is a US senator from Florida. In the following viewpoint, he maintains that if young Americans follow the "success sequence"—get a good education, find a good job, and wait until marriage to have children—they have a much better chance to achieve economic security and professional security in adulthood. Rubio asserts that the government should be doing all it can to encourage and strengthen two-parent homes and help-ing children born into single-parent families. One thing the gov-ernment can do to encourage marriage is supporting pro-family tax reforms. He discusses the impact of economic and demo-graphic changes on the American psyche, arguing that the coun-try can get its confidence and economic stability back by restor-ing the power of the American dream. Rubio says this can be accomplished through strong national leadership and the im-proved moral and social well-being of the American people.

Marco Rubio, "Strong Values for a Strong America," July 23, 2014. Rubio.Senate.gov. Courtesy of Rubio.Senate.gov.

As you read, consider the following questions:

1. According to Rubio, what percentage of children grow-ing up in poor single-parent homes will make it to the middle class or beyond?

2. What percentage of children in the United States are born to unwed mothers?

3. How many children are born to unwed mothers per hour, according to the viewpoint?

The modern world, that we all live in, tells us that success is measured by how much money we make, how much we own, or how famous we become. And I would say that, judged by this standard, my background is certainly not one of privilege. My parents immigrated here almost six decades ago with little money or any formal education. They worked service-sector jobs and had little connections to power, to in-fluence. Yet I consider myself to be a child of privilege.

Because I was raised by two parents who were married to each other, who instilled in their children the expectation that we would get our educations, that we would find fulfilling ca-reers, that we would one day get married and start families of our own. So while we weren't rich or well connected, my background, coming from a strong and stable family, gave me an enormous advantage in life—because I was taught certain values that led me to live my life in a sequence that has a proven track record of success.

The Success Sequence

In America, if you get an education, find a good job, and wait until marriage to have children, your chances of achieving economic security and professional fulfillment are incredibly high. In fact, if everyone in America lived lives that went in this order, in the order I've just outlined, some estimates are that the poverty rate would be cut by an estimated 70 percent.

But now, each element of this "success sequence" is eroding in our country. Many Americans lack the education needed for the better jobs of the 21st century. Many either can't find a good job, or have quite frankly stopped looking for one, given up. Marriage rates are on a steep decline. And a higher proportion of children are raised in single-parent homes in America than in the vast majority of developed nations.

The economic price of this erosion in the success sequence is staggering. The unemployment rate is almost twice as high for those with only high school diplomas as it is for those with bachelor's degrees, and almost three times as high for high school dropouts. Over 20 percent of children raised without both parents live in poverty long term, compared with just 2 percent of those raised in intact families. And only around 40 percent of children growing up in poor single-parent homes will ever make it to the middle class or beyond.

Restoring the American Dream

Too often in modern politics, debates about our values have been viewed as either wedges to win elections or unnecessary distractions to be avoided. But the truth is that the social and moral well-being of our people has a direct and consequential impact on their economic well-being.

And so I am grateful for this opportunity today to discuss how we can help restore the American dream by restoring the values that make it possible.

No one is born with the values crucial to the success sequence. They have to be taught to us and they have to be reinforced. Strong families are the primary and most effective teachers of these values. As the social philosopher Michael Novak once said, the family is the original and best department of health, education and welfare. It is crucial in developing the character of the young. And those efforts can be reinforced in our schools, religious institutions, civic groups and our society.

That's why reinvigorating the values behind the success sequence begins by reinvigorating the institutions that teach and reinforce these values. It is through our roles as parents, as neighbors, as volunteers and as members of faith communities that we can have the greatest influence on the social and moral well-being of our people.

Societal Breakdown and Its Consequences

Societal breakdown is not a problem that the government alone can solve, but it is also not one the government can afford to ignore. We need leaders willing to use the platform of public office to call attention to the impact societal breakdown is having on our nation.

We need leaders, in both parties, willing to acknowledge that one of the principal reasons why so many people are struggling is because too many aren't getting an education, too many aren't working, too many aren't getting married and too many are having children outside of marriage.

But we also need leaders, in both parties, willing to acknowledge that many single parents and the children they are raising are not going to have an equal opportunity to achieve a better life, unless we do something to help them.

Having more political leaders publicly recognize the link between our social well-being and our economic well-being would be enormously useful. And government reforms that promote or remove impediments to education, to work, marriage and two-parent homes would help change the direction of our country.

A Good Education

In the 21st century, a good education is not just an option, it is a necessity. And no group in America faces more impediments to a good education than children being raised by single parents, many of whom are doing a heroic job of raising their children by themselves.

If they were wealthy, they would not have this problem because they would simply pay to send their children to better schools. But lower-income parents cannot afford that. They do not have the financial means to send their kids to private and religious schools. So the government gives them no option other than sending their children to failing schools—even if just down the street are schools with higher test scores or better graduation rates.

Low-income children are the least likely to get a good education because they are the only ones forced to attend schools not of their parents' choice. In order to give them a chance at the first element of the success sequence, we need our government to give their parents the opportunity to choose the education that is right for them.

That is one of the reasons why I've proposed a tax credit that encourages contributions to scholarship granting organizations, which would distribute private school scholarships to children in need. And I've advocated for more funding and more flexibility for our nation's innovative charter schools.

A Good Job

Finding a job is the second part of the success sequence.

Helping people find work begins with an economy that creates good paying jobs. To create this growth-oriented economy, I introduced an agenda this year [2014] to enact pro-growth and pro-innovation policies, harness the power of emerging industries, and open our businesses to hundreds of millions of new customers around the world.

But helping our people find good jobs will also require reinvigorating the value of work. To do so, we must reform the way we fight poverty. Our current anti-poverty programs are incomplete. Because while they help alleviate the pain of poverty, they do not do enough to cure it.

The best cure for poverty is a good-paying job. That is why our anti-poverty programs must be reformed to incentivize work and bolster training and education.

The innovations we need to achieve these reforms will never come from the federal government, which has tried and failed for 50 years to significantly curb poverty. Only states and local communities have been able to craft and execute effective programs.

Earlier this year, I outlined my plan to transfer all federal anti-poverty spending to the states so they could design more programs tailored to the unique, localized causes of opportunity inequality—programs that will not just alleviate the pain of poverty, but also help to cure it.

Access to Higher Education

And finally, helping people attain good-paying jobs in the 21st century increasingly means having access to higher education. One of the primary reasons single mothers and their children struggle is that our current higher education system lacks the access points and the variety of options that people like them need.

That is why I have proposed reforms to make higher education more affordable and more accessible, especially for those who have to work full-time and raise a family.

This includes a series of policies aimed at promoting career and vocational opportunities, some which can begin as early as high school. . . . So that just after [they] finish high school, they don't just have a high school diploma, but they also have a job-ready industry certification that prepares them and allows them to go to work immediately.

I proposed reforms that would increase access to more affordable higher education options, such as online programs, through changes to our accreditation system—because we all know that higher education is no longer a luxury for a few, it is now a necessity for all.

A Good Marriage

After getting an education and finding a good job, the third element of the success sequence is marriage. Of course, you can achieve success without being married, but the link between marriage and economic security is undeniable. At a minimum, we should eliminate policies and programs that punish marriage.

Our current tax code penalizes marriage by hitting married couples with taxes that two otherwise identical singles would be spared from. That is why I support pro-family tax reforms that would end the marriage penalty by doubling the tax threshold for joint filers.

The final element of the success sequence is raising children in a married two-parent home. Even in my own family, of course, I have examples of children raised by one parent who have gone on to successful lives. But we also know that having an active father makes children 98 percent more likely to graduate from college and complete the first step of the success sequence.

Today a growing number of children are growing up without both parents. Fifty years ago, the percentage of children born to unwed mothers was 7 percent. Today it is 40 percent.

In just the last hour, roughly 450 children were born in America—and 180 of them were to unwed mothers. Some will go on to achieve great success in life. But as things currently stand, these children are 82 percent more likely to be in poverty during childhood. They are 44 percent less likely to earn a college degree. And they would go on to earn $4,000 less per year than the children born in married homes.

A Campaign for Children

These are figures we cannot ignore. So in addition to doing all we can to encourage and strengthen two-parent homes, we must also do all we can to help children born into these circumstances. Because if we do not, most of them will simply not have the same opportunities to succeed as children born into strong and stable families.

First, many single parents work in jobs that pay very low wages. That is why I have proposed that we increase the per-child tax credit from $1,000 to $2,500 and to make it refundable. And it's why I have proposed education reforms to help these single parents acquire the education they need for a better job, even as they work and raise their family.

Second, many single parents have jobs that come with little flexibility. As a result, their children often can't participate in sports or afterschool activities. And taking their children to a dental appointment during working hours could cost them money out of their pocket or maybe even their job.

All parents—but especially those doing it alone—need flexibility during work hours. The federal government currently prohibits the choice of paid time off as a form of compensation for overtime hours. We should end this restriction and allow our parents to spend more time with their children in return for overtime.

And third, many single parents are often overwhelmed by the financial cost of raising children all alone. We have roughly 8 million American fathers who live apart from their children. We should search for ways to help all fathers gain the financial independence necessary to financially support these children.

One reform I proposed this year was a wage enhancement credit that would bolster a low-wage earner's paycheck, thus encouraging work over dependence. We know that a working father is much more likely to support his children financially, which also makes him likelier to be an active and positive influence in their lives.

A View on Same-Sex Marriage

Now, I know that given the current cultural debates in our country, many expect that a speech on values would necessarily touch upon issues like same-sex marriage and abortion.

These are important issues and they relate to deeply held beliefs and deeply divisive ideas.

We should acknowledge that our history is marred by discrimination against gays and lesbians. There was once a time when the federal government not only banned the hiring of gay employees, it required private contractors to identify and fire them. Some laws prohibited gays from being served in bars and restaurants. And many cities carried out law enforcement efforts targeting gay Americans.

Fortunately, we have come a long way since then. But many committed gay and lesbian couples feel humiliated by the law's failure to recognize their relationship as a marriage. And supporters of same-sex marriage argue that laws banning same-sex marriage are discrimination.

I respect their arguments. And I would concede that they pose a legitimate question for lawmakers and for society.

The Traditional Marriage Argument

But there is another side of debate. Thousands of years of human history have shown that the ideal setting for children to grow up is with a mother and a father committed to one another, living together, and sharing the responsibility of raising their children. And since traditional marriage has such an extraordinary record of success at raising children into strong and successful adults, states in our country have long elevated this institution and set it apart in our laws.

That is the definition of marriage that I personally support—not because I seek to discriminate against people who love someone of the same sex, but because I believe that the union of one man and one woman is a special relationship that has proven to be of great benefit to our society, our nation and our people, and therefore deserves to be elevated in our laws.

Today, public opinion polls show there is a growing acceptance in society of the idea that marriage should be redefined to include the union of two adults of the same sex. And as a result, a number of state legislatures have changed their laws to redefine marriage. States have always regulated marriage in America, and state legislatures have a right, a constitutional right, to change those regulations.

But that right to define and regulate marriage is a two-way street. A majority of states still have laws that define marriage as one man and one woman. In some, like my home state of Florida, voters placed that definition in our state constitution. Just as states have a right to redefine marriage to include same-sex marriage, they also have right to continue to define it as between one man and one woman.

But now, all across this country, we have judges overturning state laws and defining marriage and redefining marriage from the bench. Just last week, in my home state, a local judge overturned the decision of Florida's voters to define marriage as one man and one woman.

A Growing Intolerance

Those who support same-sex marriage have a right to lobby their state legislatures to change state laws. But Americans, like myself, who support keeping the traditional definition of marriage also have a right to work to keep the traditional definition of marriage in our laws without seeing that overturned by a judge. [Editor's note: Same-sex marriage became legal in the United States on June 26, 2015, when the Supreme Court ruled that state-level bans on same-sex marriage were unconstitutional.]

Our nation has in the past demonstrated a tremendous capacity to work through issues such as this. And I believe it will again. Doing so will require those of us who support traditional marriage to respect those who support same-sex marriage. But it will also require those who support same-sex marriage to respect those of us who support traditional marriage, for tolerance is also a two-way street.

However, today, there is a growing intolerance on this issue . . . intolerance toward those who continue to support traditional marriage.

We have seen the push to remove the CEO [chief executive officer] of Mozilla because, in 2008, he made a small donation to support Proposition 8 in California, which would have upheld the traditional definition of marriage. We have seen the CEO of Starbucks tell a shareholder who supports traditional marriage that he should sell his shares and invest in some other company. And we've seen Chick-fil-A attacked and boycotted due to its CEO giving an honest answer to a question regarding his deeply held religious beliefs.

And I promise you that even before this speech is over, I will be attacked as a hater, a bigot or someone who is anti-gay.

This intolerance in the name of tolerance is hypocrisy.

Supporting the definition of marriage as one man and one woman is not anti-gay, it is pro-traditional marriage. And if support for traditional marriage is bigotry, then Barack Obama was a bigot until just before the 2012 election.

The Issue of Abortion

Abortion involves another even more fundamental moral question. It is a difficult question because it involves two competing rights: a woman's right to make choices regarding her own body versus the right of an unborn human being to live.

The decision to abort or not to abort is one that is deeply personal and emotionally painful: a 14-year-old girl who is pregnant and scared, a young single woman with her whole life ahead of her who simply doesn't feel ready to have a child. We should not pretend that if we or someone we love were facing this decision that it would be an easy one.

Those who argue that it is a woman's right to make that choice point out that it's the woman who must carry the

Senator Marco Rubio

On November 2, 2010, [Marco] Rubio defeated Governor Charlie Crist and Kendrick Meek, a Democrat, to win the Senate seat in Florida. Rubio won 50 percent of the votes. Rubio quickly made his presence felt in the Senate and became a prominent Republican leader. In February of 2013, he was chosen to deliver a Republican response to President Barack Obama's State of the Union address. In this speech, Rubio advocated a smaller government, lower taxes, and more responsible economic laws and policies. Later that year, he introduced the Foreign Aid Transparency and Accountability Act, designed to increase transparency of foreign aid. Rubio was considered a possible contender for the Republican nomination in the 2016 presidential election and groups supporting Rubio had raised more than $530,000 for consulting and research within the first three months of 2014.

"Marco Rubio," Gale Biography in Context, *2015.*

pregnancy. It is her alone who will face the risks of childbirth. And too often, it is her alone who will have to provide for and raise the child.

But there is another view that has to be considered too. For there is undeniably another person involved in this as well: an unborn child. This is not a statement of faith; it is a matter of medical science. And a human being has certain inalienable rights, primarily the right to live. And that is why this issue so deeply divides not just our politics, but also our families and our people.

In weighing these two options, I know where I stand: An unborn child should be welcomed into life and protected in law. It seems to me a decent, humane society will take tangible steps to help women with unwanted pregnancies even as that society defends an unborn child's right to live.

Changing Demographics

We will continue to debate these issues—and I suspect continue to be divided by them—for years to come. But I know that we are all impacted by the growing erosion of our faith in the American dream.

For over two centuries now, ours has been a nation of optimists—an optimism driven by plenty of secure middle-income jobs, an expanding middle class, intact two-parent homes and strong churches and communities. But now, a majority of Americans worry that our nation is headed in the wrong direction. Truth be told, we appear to be a people increasingly pessimistic about the future.

This crisis of confidence is driven not simply by a great recession, but by rapid changes in our society, our demographics and our economy.

Marriage and two-parent families are on the decline. One in three children in America is growing apart from their father. And the fastest growing household types are people living alone and two or more adult generations living together.

We are getting older as a people, with 10,000 Americans turning 65 years old each day. As a point of example, just 75 years ago, there were 42 working-age Americans for every retiree. Today there are only 3 workers for every retiree. In less than 20 years, there will be only 2 workers for every retiree.

And globalization and technology have fundamentally transformed our economy. We face more competition than ever from other nations. Automation and outsourcing have taken away millions of stable jobs, and our economy is not producing enough new ones to replace them. And while almost all the good-paying jobs of today require higher education, it has become costlier and harder to access that higher education.

America has faced rapid changes before. But we have never faced so many all at once. This perfect storm of simultaneous societal, demographic and economic change—it's left us pessimistic, insecure, uncertain and increasingly divided against each other.

It is an insecurity that cannot be measured by the unemployment rate or the performance of the stock market or the Dow Jones. It has to be measured by our people's confidence in the idea that gave birth to our country: that everyone deserves the chance to go as far as their dreams, work and talent will take them.

A Generous Nation

It is an idea, by the way, not grounded in a political concept but rather in a spiritual one: that every single person is born with certain inalienable rights that come from God.

The words 'One Nation Under God,' are not symbolic. They describe the purpose our founders saw for America. Virtually every other nation that was ever created to provide a homeland for people of a certain faith, ethnicity or language. But America was founded as the place where people could have the liberty to enjoy fully the rights given to them by God.

This idea, that all people have certain rights given to them by their creator, this idea has shaped our identity as a people and a country.

It is the reason that ours is the single most generous and caring nation on the planet. When the freedoms of others have been under assault, it is America that has sent its sons and daughters to fight and die on foreign battlefields. When AIDS and HIV were sweeping through Africa, it was America that stepped in to provide lifesaving medicines. And when a typhoon hit the Philippines or an earthquake hit Haiti, it was our navy that was first on the scene and our charities that continue to help those in need.

It is a legacy that is simply unrivaled by any other great power in all of human history.

But the belief that our rights come from God is also the reason why equality of opportunity so deeply defines us here at home. Because we don't just believe it is right for everyone to get a fair chance to get ahead, we believe it is everyone's *God-given* right.

America is indeed an exceptional nation. But it would be foolish to believe that all we have we owe solely to ourselves. For we are also a blessed people, blessed by a vast and fertile land protected by two vast oceans on either side, blessed with natural resources and natural beauty, and blessed with an innovative and creative people—a collection of go-getters who came here from all over the world and placed a man on the moon and the World Wide Web at your fingertips.

Through our compassion and through our commitment to equality of opportunity, America has been a light to the world. We have honored the blessings bestowed on us by God by adhering to the ancient admonition, "For everyone to whom much is given, from him much will be required." And God has continued to bless us in return.

Now we are called, as each generation before us was, to further this task.

A Call to Unity

Our current president has chosen to divide our people for the purpose of political gain. It is hard to believe that the state senator from Illinois who gave a stirring call to unity at the Democratic convention in 2004 is the same person who today never passes up an opportunity to pit us against each other.

But at our core, that is not who we are as a people. We are diverse and we are opinionated. And our freedoms allow us to openly and heatedly debate our differences in ways other nations discourage or even prohibit. But we are united by a common value. For while our nation may be divided on the best way to achieve equality of opportunity, we all believe in the goal of equality of opportunity.

And so it troubles us, it troubles us, that now equal opportunity eludes too many of our people. But what we need are not leaders who will exploit this anxiety. We need leaders who will explain to us why this is happening because they do not have enough education and therefore they can't find jobs, because so many are being raised in broken homes, and because too many face the challenges of providing for their children as single parents all by themselves.

And we need leaders that provide us with answers that will address these problems by fixing our education system and improving our economy, by highlighting the importance of marriage and two-parent homes, and by helping children raised in broken families and parents struggling with the burden of single parenting.

A Return to the American Dream

No plan to restore the American dream is complete without addressing these things. We will never improve our people's economic well-being without also improving their moral and social well-being.

The challenge for those of us in politics is that, while our role is important, we alone can't do this. There is no magic five-point plan for restoring marriage. There's no innovative program that will instill the value of education and hard work. There's no law we can pass to make men better fathers and husbands.

The ultimate responsibility for our social well-being rests on us as a people. What we do as parents, neighbors and members of a church, a charity or community will often have a greater impact on our nation's future than what we do as voters or even as a senator.

A strong America is not possible without strong Americans—a people formed by the values necessary for success, the values of education and hard work, strong marriages and empowered parents. These are values that made us the greatest nation ever, and these are the values that will lead us to a future even better than our past.

"*[In June 2012, the Department of Health and Human Services] released the results of several years of research about the performance of marriage programs, and it indicates that the Bush-era effort to encourage Americans (straight ones, at least) to walk down the aisle has been a serious flop.*"

The Government Should Not Be Promoting Marriage

Stephanie Mencimer

Stephanie Mencimer is a journalist. In the following viewpoint, she reviews recent findings from the Department of Health and Human Services that federal initiatives to push marriage have been colossal failures. Mencimer notes that millions of dollars, much of it diverted from welfare programs, were allocated to questionable programs that sponsored date nights, marriage education classes, and romance workshops. Although the evidence is clear that the programs are not working, many of them continue to be funded, bolstered by support from conservative lawmakers and President Barack Obama. The only change is that some of the biggest flops have been eliminated in favor of more conventional approaches to promoting marriage and strengthening relationships.

As you read, consider the following questions:

1. According to Mencimer, in what year was the Healthy Marriages Initiative launched?
2. What is the Building Healthy Families program, according to the author?
3. How much money did the US Congress allocate to healthy marriage and fatherhood-related programs in 2013?

With congressional Republicans beating the drum about profligate and wasteful government spending, they may want to take a hard look at a federal program pushed by a host of top GOPers during the [George W.] Bush era and re-authorized in late 2010, as the Republican deficit craze took hold. Originally championed by Republican lawmakers including Iowa Sen. Chuck Grassley, former Pennsylvania Sen. Rick Santorum, and current Kansas Gov. Sam Brownback, a federal initiative to promote marriage as a cure for poverty dumped hundreds of millions of dollars into programs that either had no impact or a negative effect on the relationships of the couples who took part, according to recent research by the Department of Health and Human Services (HHS).

The Healthy Marriage Initiative

Launched during the Bush administration at the behest of evangelical Christian activists and with the aid of congressional Republicans, the federal Healthy Marriage Initiative was designed to help low-income couples put a little sizzle in their marriages and urge poor unmarried parents to tie the knot, in the hopes that marriage would enhance their finances and get them off the federal dole. Starting in 2006, millions of dollars were hastily distributed to grantees to further this poverty reduction strategy. The money went to such enterprises as "Laugh Your Way America," a program run by a non-Spanish-speaking Wisconsin minister who used federal dollars to offer "Laugh Your Way to a Better Marriage" seminars to Latinos. It funded Rabbi Stephen Baars, a British rabbi who'd been giving his trademarked "Bliss" marriage seminars to upper-middle-class Jews in Montgomery County, Maryland, for years. With the help of the federal government, he brought his program to inner-city DC for the benefit of African American single moms.

The marriage money was diverted from the Temporary Assistance for Needy Families program (formerly known as welfare), and much of it went to religious groups that went to work trying to combat the divorce rate in their communities by sponsoring date nights and romance workshops. In some cities, the local grantees used their federal funds to recruit professional athletes to make public service announcements touting the benefits of marriage. Women's groups were especially critical of the marriage initiative, largely because it was the baby of Wade Horn, a controversial figure who Bush installed at HHS as the head of the Administration for Children and Families and the administration's official "marriage czar."

Before joining the Bush administration, Horn, a conservative psychologist, had helmed the National Fatherhood Initiative, where he attacked what he called the "we hate marriage" elites and infuriated women's groups by defending the Southern Baptist Convention's proclamation that women should "submit" to their husbands' "servant leadership." Horn believed that federal poverty programs should be vehicles for marriage promotion, once proposing that the federal government exclude unmarried people from anti-poverty programs like Head Start and from public housing. Horn's deputy was Chris Gersten (husband of former Bush Labor secretary Linda

Chavez), who implemented the program and who is a strong believer in the value of "relationship education" in combating the social scourge of the disintegrating traditional family.

"A middle-class couple with $100,000 a year that's having trouble in their marriage, they can go out and spend $200 or $300 or $400 to get some classes that help them," he explains, "But a poor couple isn't going to spend the rent money on relationship classes."

Marriage Programs Prove to Be Flops

Studies show that relationship classes can be helpful for white, middle-class couples, but when the federal government started dumping millions of poverty dollars into marriage education, there was virtually no research on how such programs would fare with poor, inner-city single moms. Now, though, the data is in, and it doesn't look good for proponents of taxpayer-funded marriage education. This month [June 2012], HHS released the results of several years of research about the performance of the marriage programs, and it indicates that the Bush-era effort to encourage Americans (straight ones, at least) to walk down the aisle has been a serious flop.

At a recent conference sponsored by the HHS Office of Planning, Research and Evaluation, researchers looking at various aspects of the marriage initiative presented their findings. They had nothing but bad news.

Take the Building Healthy Families program, which targeted unmarried but romantically involved couples who were either new parents or expecting a baby. The program, tested in Baltimore and seven other cities, offered participants many weeks of marriage education classes that focused on improving their relationships with the hopes that this would also help their children. Three years later, researchers reported that the program had produced precisely zero impact on the quality of the couples' relationships, rates of domestic violence, or the involvement of fathers with their children. In fact, couples in the eight pilot programs around the country actually broke up more frequently than those in a control group who didn't get the relationship program. The program also prompted a drop in the involvement of fathers and the percentage who provided financial support.

In a few bright spots, married couples who participated in a government-funded relationship class reported being somewhat happier and having slightly warmer relationships with their partners. But the cost of this slight bump in happiness in the Supporting Healthy Marriage program was a whopping $7,000 to $11,500 per couple. Imagine how much happier the couples would have been if they'd just been handed with cash. Indeed, feeling flush might have helped them stay married. After all, the only social program ever to show documented success in impacting the marriage rates of poor people came in 1994, when the state of Minnesota accidentally reduced the divorce rate among poor black women by allowing them to keep some of their welfare benefits when they went to work rather than cutting them off. During the three-year experiment and for a few years afterward, the divorce rate for black women in the state fell 70 percent. The positive effects on kids also continued for several years.

Pleading for Time

Gersten isn't persuaded by the research on the federal marriage initiative—at least not yet. He thinks the programs just need more time to work out the kinks. "I think in the long run you can't justify funding programs that don't show results, but I don't think a couple years is adequate," he says, acknowledging that the original marriage grantees often had trouble finding participants to offer their services to.

"There's no demand," he laments. "The culture isn't saying, 'You just had a baby, you need to figure out how to form

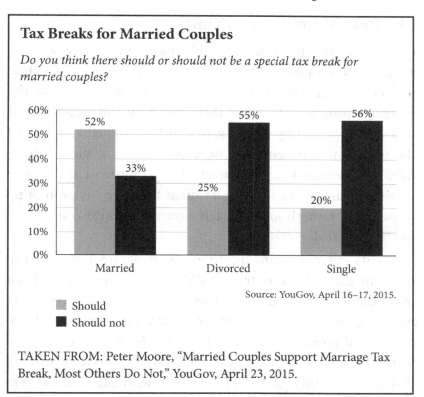

Tax Breaks for Married Couples

Do you think there should or should not be a special tax break for married couples?

Source: YouGov, April 16–17, 2015.

■ Should
■ Should not

TAKEN FROM: Peter Moore, "Married Couples Support Marriage Tax Break, Most Others Do Not," YouGov, April 23, 2015.

a bond with the father.' The culture did say that until the '60s." Gersten says that the culture of liberation, birth control, the sexual revolution, and, of course, the rise of the welfare state has "led to an out-of-wedlock birth rate in the black community of 60 to 70 percent. It's devastating." So he thinks the government needs to keep pushing marriage.

Given the underwhelming track record of the federal marriage program, it would seem a ripe target for GOP budget hawks, especially given that many of the original proponents of the program are no longer in Congress to defend it. Instead, in November 2010, Congress allocated another $150 million for healthy marriage and fatherhood-related programs, with another $150 million budgeted for 2013. And this fall HHS doled out $120 million worth of grants.

The Role of President Obama

Oddly enough, the program might have faded away without an unlikely supporter: President [Barack] Obama. According to Gersten, the administration initially wanted to retool the marriage programs to focus them more on job training. But in a deal brokered by Grassley, one of the original sponsors of the program, and Sen. Max Baucus (D-Mont.), the marriage initiative remained mostly intact, though more of the money originally earmarked for it was shifted to programs promoting responsible fatherhood. Gersten says the administration approved the deal.

In its current form, the marriage program looks a little different under Obama than it did under Bush. Many of the more dubious marriage programs, including "Laugh Your Way America," did not receive further funding, for instance. While faith-based groups continue to receive federal money, the ones in the program tend to be more established service providers that combine their marriage offerings with other social services for low-income people, such as employment help. When the administration issued the grant requirements, it insisted on the programs having a strong employment component along with the Oprah [Winfrey]–style relationship classes.

Ron Haskins, a marriage program supporter who is a former adviser to Bush on welfare issues and a senior fellow at the Brookings Institution, thinks Obama did the right thing. He points out that research on poverty programs beloved by liberals, such as Head Start, doesn't look so good either, but that doesn't mean the government should simply get rid of it. "When there's tremendous pressure on the budget, there is a reason for reducing the spending," he says. "The exception is, if it's a new program you ought to try to figure out if you can improve it." Haskins notes that in the grand scheme of the federal budget, the marriage program is but a blip. "We don't spend a lot of money on these programs. [We spend] $7 billion on Head Start, but not even a $100 million on these [marriage] programs."

> *"Despite how thoroughly we've embraced the more romantic notion that marriage should be a partnership of soul mates in our popular culture, we remain remarkably, well, married to the idea that the institution can be a utilitarian silver bullet that solves the underlying structural problems of our economy."*

New Benefits of Marriage Study Actually Hints at the Horrors of Middle Age

Maya Dusenbery

Maya Dusenbery is a writer and an editor. In the following viewpoint, she reviews recent research that finds that marriage appears to increase levels of life satisfaction, particularly during the difficult period of middle age. Dusenbery suggests that marriage seems to be beneficial in addressing many of the stresses of middle age, especially social isolation, economic struggles, and the challenges of child-rearing. She also points out that existing economic structures and work policies cater to two-parent part-

nerships, making it even more difficult for single parents or those in relationships outside the conventional two-parent paradigm. She argues that society should stop pushing marriage as a silver bullet to economic stress and focus on addressing economic inequalities that impact all relationships.

As you read, consider the following questions:

1. According to Dusenbery, what percentage of adults in the United States are unmarried?

2. When does research pinpoint as the time when the benefits of being married are most evident?

3. How much money does Dusenbery assert the United States has wasted over the past decade on federal marriage promotion programs?

Marriage has long been linked to greater happiness, health, and well-being, at least in wealthy, Western cultures. Previous studies, though, could only hazard a correlation, and researchers warned of a likely significant selection bias at play. But a new paper, published by the National Bureau of Economic Research and based primarily on data from the United Kingdom, suggests that there's a real causal effect of getting married.

Even after controlling for premarital well-being levels, as well as other potentially confounding factors, marriage appears to increase life satisfaction, beyond the honeymoon period, and particularly during the slump in happiness that often accompanies middle age. The effect seems to have less to do with the legal institution than with the relationship; the benefit of cohabitating is almost as large. Noting that those who describe their partner as their best friend see double the boost in well-being, the researchers conclude that it is the friendship offered by a spouse or long-term partner that's most important.

"Marriage, in a sense, is a super friendship," the study's co-author Shawn Grover explained to the *Huffington Post*.

Unsurprisingly, much media coverage of this research has taken a reductive and prescriptive tone, best epitomized by the *New York Times*' misleading headline: "Study Finds More Reasons to Get and Stay Married." In reality, nobody is suggesting there's any benefit to staying in an unhappy marriage, which has consistently been shown to be at least as bad—and usually worse—for your physical and mental health as being unmarried. And analyses of survey data, particularly on subjective, self-reported well-being measures, should always be taken with a grain of salt. "Averages always obscure important variations," says Stephanie Coontz, the director of research at the Council on Contemporary Families. "And that's especially true today, when there is no such thing as a typical marriage or a typical single person, and there are greater differences within each family type than there are between them."

Plus, considering the privileged space marriage still occupies in our popular imagination and socioeconomic structures, this new study starts to look about as surprising as one showing that the world's a little bit easier to navigate if you're right-handed.

After all, it's impossible to control for the enormous pressure people feel to get married in many cultures. Despite the fact that in the United States nearly half of adults are unmarried and more than a quarter of all households consist of only one person, there's a veritable romantic industrial complex—aimed especially at women—reminding us to couple up and settle down before we die alone. As a 2009 study exploring the stigma felt by never-married women in their late 20s to mid-30s put it: "The idealization of marriage and child-rearing remains strong, pervasive, and largely unquestioned." And while single people often invest in other close relationships—indeed, they typically have more active social lives than their married counterparts—we have yet to support alternative family structures. As my friend Samhita Mukhopadhyay, author of *Outdated: Why Dating Is Ruining Your Love Life*, says, "These alternatives are still very much at the margins of the dominant organizing principle of our society, which is the nuclear family—or heteronormative romantic structures."

It's not surprising, then, that the benefits of being married are most evident during middle age, when the marriage rate peaks—and with it, the peer pressure to join the club. Furthermore, as Natalia Sarkisian and Naomi Gerstel argue in their book *Nuclear Family Values, Extended Family Lives: The Power of Race, Class, and Gender*, marriage is a fairly "greedy" institution—married people tend to invest less time in their relationships with friends, extended family, and the broader community. Though it's not something Sarkisian and Gerstel have looked at specifically in their research, it seems likely that this domestic nesting would be especially acute in middle age, when career and child-rearing duties pile up.

And while its effects may be felt by those who remain single and find their support networks weakened as their married friends become less available, it hardly serves the married that well either, as recent articles on the difficulty of making and maintaining friendships in (married) middle age attest. No wonder people whose spouses also happen to be their best friends get such a greater benefit from marriage than others. For some, this particular "super-friend" may well be one of the *only* close friends they see with any regularity—it helps to really, *really* like them.

Looked at from that angle, the fact that marrying your best friend seems to make middle age "slightly less terrible" (as the headline of the *Washington Post*'s coverage of the study sardonically boasts) seems less a ringing endorsement of marriage than an indictment of the way many of us spend our middle age—in socially isolated domestic units, each consumed with the nearly impossible task of balancing work and family, made bearable only by having a close friend in the trenches with us.

Perhaps nowhere is this more true than in the U.S., where, despite the growing diversity of our families, our economic structures and work policies stubbornly cater to two-parent partnerships—and don't even properly support those. Granted, some of the "stresses of middle age" that can be eased by marital friendship are probably inevitable—raising a child, caring for a dying parent, or facing the first evidence of your own impending mortality, for example, will never be easy. But, in the U.S., we seem to have all but given up on the possibility that at least one key challenge of this life stage—the fact that career and family obligations often peak at the exact same time—could, conceivably, be collectively solved. Instead, we accept ever longer work hours, stagnating wages, astronomical child care costs, and laughable family leave policies, and then find, unsurprisingly, that more than half of working parents say it is difficult for them to balance their job and home responsibilities.

In such a context, the support offered by a spouse is not just emotional but also, often, material—a second income, another adult to pick up the kids from school, double the sick days, a much-needed benefits package. It is, in fact, even possible to estimate the exact financial price of remaining single in the U.S.

Of course, not so long ago, before the feminist movement ushered more women into the workforce and led to a convergence of gender roles, the benefits of marriage were imagined in even more crassly utilitarian terms. Economist Gary Becker argued that through marriage, women gained a breadwinner, and men were provided a housewife. And despite how thoroughly we've embraced the more romantic notion that marriage should be a partnership of soul mates in our popular culture, we remain remarkably, well, married to the idea that the institution can be a utilitarian silver bullet that solves the underlying structural problems of our economy—or, more accurately, a Band-Aid that masks the need to tackle them.

This is particularly true of the rhetoric that surrounds marriages among the least privileged. Conservatives wring their hands over the marriage gap between the rich and poor and claim that single mothers, who are disproportionately likely to live in poverty, need husbands rather than a living wage and a more robust social safety net. Last summer [in 2014], a Heritage Foundation panel concluded that if women would just get married, income inequality could be eliminated. And this is an idea we've tested by wasting nearly a billion dollars over the past decade on federal marriage-promotion programs that have utterly failed.

Meanwhile, on the opposite end of the income spectrum, the debate about "having it all" (largely sparked by Anne-Marie Slaughter's *Atlantic* piece a couple of years ago)—which, in a sane world, might have led to a widespread movement to reduce work hours and join everyone else in enacting mandatory paid family leave—seems to have quietly wound down with the tepid conclusion that *nobody* can have it all. Apparently, the best we can hope for is a good marriage to make things a tiny bit easier. As Ruth Bader Ginsburg said in a recent interview with Katie Couric: "You can't have it all all at once. Over my lifespan, I think I have had it all, but in given periods in time, things were rough. And if you have a caring life partner, you help the other person when that person needs it."

Even when we're not making such an explicitly economic case for coupledom, we prescribe marriage as though finding a life partner were as easy as flipping a switch. See, for example, the *New York Times*' take-away from this latest study: "Overall, the research comes to a largely optimistic conclusion. People have the capacity to increase their happiness levels and avoid falling deep into midlife crisis by finding support in long-term relationships." As always, in our up-by-your-bootstraps, self-help culture, the only thing standing in the way of your happiness is you.

Never mind that, as this study shows, *who* you marry is pretty damn important. And never mind that it takes time to cultivate good relationships, romantic or otherwise, temporary or lifelong—and time is something that's in short supply. Indeed, the cruelest irony here might be that the low-income Americans most targeted by our marriage-promotion efforts have the least control over their time. When you're napping in your car in between multiple part-time, low-wage jobs, I'm not sure when exactly you're supposed to kiss enough frogs to find your very own "super-friend."

If we truly took to heart the importance of close social ties to our well-being—which the research certainly supports—instead of pushing marriage as a means of weathering the stresses caused by our current economy, we might build a better one that allows for all types of relationships to flourish in the first place.

Periodical and Internet Sources Bibliography

The following articles have been selected to supplement the diverse views presented in this chapter.

Rebecca Adams	"New Study Says You Should Marry Your Best Friend," *Huffington Post*, January 9, 2015.
Julie Baumgardner	"Why the Government Should Promote Relationship Skills," Institute for Family Studies, January 15, 2014.
Philip N. Cohen	"This 'Supporting Healthy Marriage,' I Do Not Think It Means What You Think It Means," *Family Inequality*, April 7, 2014.
Bryce Covert	"Romney's Solution to Poverty: Poor People Should Get Married," *ThinkProgress*, January 29, 2015.
Taryn Hillin	"Hundreds of Millions Spent Promoting Marriage Hasn't Helped at All: Study," *Huffington Post*, February 10, 2014.
Kimberly Howard and Richard V. Reeves	"The Marriage Effect: Money or Parenting?," Brookings Institution, September 4, 2014.
Olga Khazan	"The Plight of Single Moms—and the Policies That Would Help," *Atlantic*, January 14, 2014.
Jenny Kutner	"Indiana Lawmaker Proposes 'Office of Marriage Promotion,'" *Salon*, February 3, 2015.
Laurie C. Maldonado and Rense Nieuwenhuis	"The Social Policy Context of Single Parent Families," *Policy & Politics*, February 26, 2015.
Claire Cain Miller	"Study Finds More Reasons to Get and Stay Married," *New York Times*, January 8, 2015.

CHAPTER 4

What Policies May Help Single-Parent Families?

Chapter Preface

On November 20, 2014, President Barack Obama announced a series of executive actions to address the thorny issue of immigration reform in the United States. Under the administration's plan, officially known as Deferred Action for Parents of Americans and Lawful Permanent Residents or Deferred Action for Parental Accountability (DAPA), undocumented workers that fit into certain categories would be issued work documents, which would defer deportation processes and allow them to stay in the country. Many of these protections would be extended to the parents of children who are US citizens or legal residents, thereby keeping many two-parent families together while the parents work toward US citizenship.

President Obama viewed his plan not only as a humane act but also as essential to the country's economic self-interest. "Are we a nation that accepts the cruelty of ripping children from their parents' arms, or are we a nation that values families and works together to keep them together?" he asked in his remarks to the nation.

The president's plan generated a firestorm of political controversy. Republican lawmakers quickly took him to task for acting unilaterally and not working with the US Congress to find a compromise immigration reform plan. As then House Speaker John Boehner suggested in a statement about President Obama's executive order, "The American people want both parties to focus on solving problems together; they don't support unilateral action from a president who is more interested in partisan politics than working with the people's elected representatives. That is not how American democracy works."

However, the American people largely agreed with the specifics of DAPA. In a CNN/ORC poll released on November 26,

2014, about 50 percent of poll respondents believed that the plan was correct, while 22 percent said that it didn't go far enough. Despite the generally favorable reaction to the specifics of the plan, a majority of respondents (56 percent) opposed the way the president had gone about getting the job done through unilateral executive action.

Opponents of immigration reform and the president's executive action launched a number of legal challenges to DAPA in the hopes of killing it before it could take effect. On December 4, a lawsuit was filed on behalf of seventeen states to halt the immigration program. The states contended that the proposed immigration reforms in DAPA could make it easier for non-US citizens to vote and would result in higher rates of voter fraud. By the end of January 2015, several more states joined the lawsuit.

On February 16, 2015, a federal district court in Texas issued an injunction against President Obama's executive order on immigration. Judge Andrew S. Hanen issued a temporary injunction blocking the program from going into effect until the lawsuit was fully resolved. In his opinion, he made it clear that the president does not have the authority to ignore the will of the US Congress and make up his own laws.

White House press secretary Josh Earnest criticized Judge Hanen's decision, claiming that the president did have the authority to act. "The Supreme Court and Congress have made clear that the federal government can set priorities in enforcing our immigration laws—which is exactly what the president did when he announced commonsense policies to fix our broken immigration system," he stated in his remarks.

The Obama administration appealed the court's injunction. In November 2015, the US Court of Appeals for the Fifth Circuit agreed with the decision to invoke the injunction. The appeals court also concurred that Texas and other states that sued the president over DAPA had legal standing to challenge DAPA's constitutionality in federal court. As a result, DAPA could not be implemented until further notice.

The impact of immigration reform on single-parent families is one of the topics considered in the following chapter. Other viewpoints in the chapter assess the benefits of sentencing reform, expanded family planning and contraception efforts, more educational opportunities, and a higher minimum wage for single parents.

> "It is not just marriage that improves a
> child's life chances, but family planning
> as well."

Family Planning Is Essential to Strengthening Families and Helping Children

Isabel V. Sawhill

Isabel V. Sawhill is an author and codirector of the Center on Children and Families at the Brookings Institution. In the following viewpoint, she maintains that better family planning could be a huge benefit to both families and children because it allows parents to delay having children until they are financially and emotionally ready. With parents able to determine the size of their families and plan the timing of when they have children, couples are better positioned to address the needs of children in today's society. This results in better educational outcomes for children, leading to higher incomes and professional achievement as adults. Clearly, there is a significant societal benefit to encouraging and facilitating improved family planning, particularly in low-income communities. Sawhill suggests that society needs to do a better job educating women about contraceptive choices and providing birth control at no cost to the recipient to help families in that effort.

As you read, consider the following questions:

1. According to the author, what percentage of African American children were born outside marriage in 2012?

2. What percentage of cohabiting parents will have split up by the time the child is five years old?

3. What reality TV show does Sawhill identify as being responsible for one-third of the reduction in the teen birth rate in 2009–2010?

Fifty years ago, in 1965, [U.S. senator] Daniel Patrick Moynihan presciently warned that the breakdown of the family was becoming a key source of disadvantage in the African American community. He received intense criticism at the time. Yet the trends he identified have not gone away. Indeed, they have "trickled up" to encompass not just a much larger fraction of the African American community but a large swath of the white community as well. Still, the racial gaps remain large. The proportion of black children born outside marriage was 72 percent in 2012, while the white proportion was 36 percent.

The effects on children of the increase in single parents is no longer much debated. They do less well in school, are less likely to graduate, and are more likely to be involved in crime, teen pregnancy, and other behaviors that make it harder to succeed in life. Not every child raised by a single parent will suffer from the experience, but, on average, a lone parent has fewer resources—both time and money—with which to raise a child. Poverty rates for single-parent families are five times those for married-parent families. The growth of such families since 1970 has increased the overall child poverty rate by about 5 percentage points (from 20 to 25 percent).

Rates of social mobility are also lower for these families. Harvard researcher Raj Chetty and his colleagues find that the incidence of single parenthood in a community is one of the most powerful predictors of geographic differences in social mobility in the United States. And our research at the Brookings Institution also shows that social mobility is much higher for the children of continuously married parents than for those who grow up with discontinuously married or never-married parents. Moynihan was especially concerned about the large number of boys growing up in "broken families, dominated by women, never acquiring any stable relationship to male authority, never acquiring any set of rational expectations about the future. . . ." Recent research suggests that boys are indeed more affected than girls by the lack of a male role model in the family. If true, this sets the stage for a cycle of poverty in which mother-headed families produce boys who go on to father their own children outside marriage.

But what does all of this have to do with education? Rates of unwed childbearing and divorce are much lower among well educated than among less educated women. The proportion of first births that occur outside of marriage is only 12 percent for those who are college graduates but 58 percent for everyone else. So more and better education is one clear path to reducing unwed parenthood and the growth of single-parent families in the future.

Why Does Education Matter?

Education clearly improves the economic prospects of men and women, making them more marriageable. But the commonly heard argument that the declining economic prospects of men are the culprit in this story about unwed births is too simple. It doesn't explain why some young adults feel they are too poor to marry but believe they can afford to raise a child. Or why marriage was so much more prevalent in an earlier era, when everyone had fewer resources.

One reason that education may help to increase marriage rates is that the better educated tend to have more egalitarian gender roles, which makes marriage more appealing, especially to women. For women who work outside the home, flexible parenting arrangements help them avoid having to "do it all" and the resentment that engenders.

Finally, and critically, in my view, the better educated are much more successful at avoiding the arrival of a baby before they are in a committed relationship and ready to be parents. An unwed birth, not divorce, is now the most common entry point into single parenthood. Although the mother may be living with the child's father at the time of the birth, these cohabiting relationships are very fragile. By the time the child is age five, about half of cohabiting parents will have split up. More education sharply reduces the drifting into unstable relationships and the single parenthood that this often produces.

The relationship between education and the ability to plan a family goes in both directions. If young adults had more education, there would be less drifting and fewer unwed births. And if there were better family planning, young people could finish their schooling. There would then be more purposeful parenthood, more children ready for school when they enroll, and, later on, better educated young adults making better parenting decisions of their own.

Education Out of School

While education is critically important, if we focus only on what can be done during the schooling years to improve educational outcomes, we will likely fail. Not all human-capital development occurs in a classroom; some of it occurs in the home. Children from underprivileged backgrounds typically start school way behind their more fortunate peers. These gaps tend to persist as children move through school and pose enormous challenges to teachers and other school personnel. We need to focus attention on what happens to a child long before he or she starts school.

Starting earlier means focusing on what occurs before a child enters any form of schooling, including a pre-K program. Let's call the prior period pre-pre-K, a term coined by my colleague Richard Reeves. It spans from infancy through toddlerhood. During this period, development is rapid, and the home environment looms large. The quality of parenting matters a lot. Some parenting or home-visiting programs have improved the quality of parenting and thus a child's later outcomes, including readiness for school. But not all such programs are effective, and they face an uphill struggle: The evidence suggests that class differences in parenting styles are growing, rather than diminishing.

The developmental stage prior to infancy is the prenatal period, from conception to birth. Scientists have just begun to diagram the underlying mechanics, but the consequences of events during pregnancy are numerous and clear. In a study published in the *British Journal of Psychiatry*, for example, the most anxious 15 percent of participating mothers were twice as likely to deliver children with behavioral concerns like ADHD [attention deficit/hyperactivity disorder]; the effect remained even after controlling for the mothers' postnatal stress. Another study found that prenatally stressed nine-year-olds have less gray-matter density in regions associated with cognitive function. David Figlio, with three other researchers, has examined the effects of prenatal health on school success, using 14,000 pairs of Florida twins. The twins with lower birth weights, a proxy for worse prenatal health, scored consistently lower on reading and math tests through 8th grade. The twins' gender, race, and socioeconomic class did not change the results, nor did their schools' quality.

Further upstream still are the circumstances of the parents-to-be. Have they finished school? Are they emotionally mature and financially independent? Did they choose to have children with someone they can envision living with in a committed relationship for the time it takes to raise the child? Did they plan to have the child? In short, are they reasonably well prepared to take on the most important task any adult ever undertakes?

In *Generation Unbound*, I show that a large fraction of young adults are "drifting" into sex and parenthood without having thought very much, if at all, about these questions. About half of new parents under 30 are unmarried (although often in cohabiting relationships). Among these unmarried parents-to-be, more than 70 percent began the pregnancy unintentionally, according to their own reports. Many are still in school (either high school or college); 21 percent of nonmarital births are to women under age 20.

When unmarried parents are asked why they haven't married, many say that it is because they can't "afford" to. Why they think it takes less money to raise a child than to marry is a major puzzle. It seems that marriage, while still celebrated in the abstract, is viewed as a distant goal—the capstone not the cornerstone of a successful life, as Johns Hopkins professor Andrew Cherlin notes. In the meantime, children are being raised in environments marked by inadequate resources and unstable relationships. No wonder that when they get to school, children are often not ready to learn. Schools are asked to compensate for the failure of children's first teachers—their parents—to instill in them the attitudes and habits, the love of learning, and the ability to interact constructively with others that success in school requires.

Reconnecting Marriage and Parenting

Can we encourage more planning and less drifting among young adults and perhaps bring back marriage, or at least a long-term committed relationship, as the standard precursor to bearing and raising children in the U.S.?

No one knows. According to some, there is a dearth of so-called marriageable men, defined as those who are employed. But there is an even greater dearth of marriageable women, defined as not having children from a previous relationship: Using these metrics, there are only 62 marriageable women for every 100 marriageable men. But there are reasons to be optimistic and reasons to be pessimistic about the future.

On the optimistic side, well-educated elites are still marrying. This model could eventually trickle down to the less well educated. Marriage still has many benefits for both adults and children. Moreover, marriage is a legally and socially supported institution in our culture and an integral part of many people's religious faith.

On the pessimistic side, major demographic trends, once they gain a certain momentum, are hard to reverse. The youngest generation is marrying less than older ones, suggesting that the retreat from marriage will continue. Other advanced countries are also seeing a decline in marriage, suggesting the trend has little to do with policies specific to the U.S. And opportunities for women that enable them to support themselves and establish identities separate from those of wife and mother are still increasing. Perhaps most distressing, single parenthood may replicate itself intergenerationally by reducing the life chances of children, especially boys with absent fathers.

What might we do to ensure that more children are born to adults who are ready to be parents and in a stable and committed relationship?

Different Approaches

There seem to be two schools of thought about this. Liberals contend that single parents are here to stay and need more assistance. Conservatives want to restore marriage as the primary institution for raising children. I do not disagree with their goal, but we have no real agenda for achieving it. Marriage education programs and efforts to make taxes and benefit programs more marriage friendly have not moved the needle much, if at all. For example, President George W. Bush

Family Planning

Family planning and control over reproduction emerged in the early twentieth century and throughout the twenty-first century as both a personal choice for families and a political issue for governments. By the middle of the twentieth century, population growth caused serious strain on resources for some governments, and the landmark 1978 State of World Population report from the United Nations highlighted the need for government policies to address population concerns. It became apparent that family planning, reproductive health, maternal mortality, and infant mortality were inexorably linked to concerns about overpopulation.

In the United States, Margaret Sanger (1879—1966), a public health nurse in the first two decades of the twentieth century, founded the American Birth Control League, which later became Planned Parenthood [Federation of America], to address basic reproductive education and contraceptive device access. In Great Britain, Marie Stopes (1880–1958) opened the first birth control clinic in the UK in 1921. Family planning was thwarted by federal and state laws in the United States and national law in other countries that made dissemination of contraceptive information or devices a crime. Family planning was, and still is, [primarily] a women's rights issue. Reproductive health and education, access to birth control, and the right to choose when to have children have been central points in many women's movements worldwide since Sanger and Stopes began their family planning practices. By the twenty-first century, acceptance of family planning has become more widespread, though still controversial among some cultures and religions.

"Family Planning," Gale Global Issues in Context, 2015.

launched a Healthy Marriage Initiative in 2002 that funded programs to encourage or sustain marriage among low-income families using counseling and relationship education. One carefully evaluated program, Building Strong Families, focused on unwed parents but had no effect on their marriage rates. Perhaps government is not the best source of marriage-promotion efforts. Religious and civic organizations, on the other hand, have a role to play, but they are working against some powerful trends in the other direction.

Both conservatives and liberals support strengthening the education and training system to ensure that young adults will have the kind of opportunities that will motivate them to avoid early parenthood and make marriage more likely. Especially important is making sure that well-paying jobs are available to young men, thereby making them more marriageable. More career and technical education, apprenticeships, and wage subsidies for childless individuals have all been proposed as possible contributors to this goal. Whether they will work or not to slow the growth of single-parent families remains to be seen.

My own view is that much more attention needs to be given to changing drifters into planners, that is, to encouraging young adults to think more about whether, when, and with whom to have children. Backed up by the availability of newer and much more effective forms of birth control, and reasonable educational and career opportunities for young men and women, this is a realistic goal. It should help to reconnect marriage and parenting by encouraging young adults to wait until they have met Mr. or Ms. Right before having children.

The Role of Birth Control

It is not just marriage that improves a child's life chances, but family planning as well. Once couples are able to plan together when to have children, it improves a child's education and adult earning ability. In a series of papers, University of Michigan professor Martha Bailey found that the diffusion of effective forms of birth control, such as the pill [referring to oral contraception], after legal and financial restraints on its use were lifted in the 1960s and 1970s, enabled young men and women to adjust the number and timing of their children to better reflect their preferences. This, in turn, enabled their children to obtain more education and higher incomes. Bailey suggests several mechanisms for these impacts on a child's education and income as an adult. When parents achieve their own goals, their families are smaller, which enables them to extend their own educational and labor market experiences, and to invest more time or resources in each child. In addition, there is a smaller youth cohort. This smaller cohort limits competition for public resources, including teacher time (e.g., class size) and college slots. Finally, young adults are able to delay marriage, much as the well educated are doing today, leading to better and more stable matches. Bailey finds that the increased availability and lower costs of family planning in the 1960s and 1970s produced a 2 to 3 percent increase in family income for all of the children in an affected cohort, and perhaps a 20 to 30 percent gain for those children who benefited most directly from their parents' greater access to birth control. She notes that "an important component of these income gains reflects increases in children's educational attainment."

The chief actor in this historical drama was the invention and diffusion of the pill. Now, a second family planning revolution is in the offing, led by long-acting reversible contraceptives (or LARCs), such as IUDs [intrauterine devices]. Where they have been made affordable, and women have been educated about their safety and effectiveness, usage has climbed dramatically and unintended pregnancy rates have fallen sharply. They enable women to pursue more education, to get more experience on the job, and to marry unencumbered by a child from a prior relationship. High schools and community colleges could be doing more to educate young people about their contraceptive options, but their efforts need to be supplemented with good online resources. These and popular media are proving to be effective ways of getting out new messages and information. The TV reality show *16 and Pregnant* was responsible for one-third of the reduction in the teen birth rate in 2009–10, according to a study by economists Phillip Levine, at Wellesley College, and Melissa Kearney, at the University of Maryland.

Addressing the Problem

Is birth control a magic bullet? No. There will always be some people who want a baby, even though they are not prepared to raise her, and there will always be others, who despite not being ready for parenthood, do not choose to avail themselves of the most effective and easy ways of preventing it. But I believe a lot of the discussion about the value of children in low-income communities is based on small samples of highly disadvantaged individuals and should not be extrapolated to the half of all births that are now occurring outside of marriage among the youngest generation. The hard data, as opposed to the more qualitative evidence, show that the majority of unwed births are unintended. And unintended pregnancy and birth rates are especially high among low-income and minority women. If we could lower their unintended pregnancy rates to the level experienced by college-educated women, we could reduce the proportion of children born outside of marriage by 25 percent.

Of course, we should work on expanding educational and job opportunities at the same time to increase the motivation to avoid early pregnancy, but I know of no other approach that could have as large an effect on unwed childbearing as better birth control and at the same time save money for the government. Specifically, we need to educate women about their contraceptive choices (many don't know about IUDs, and those who do are often misinformed about their safety and effectiveness), make them available at no cost to the recipient, and train the medical community on the best clinical practices. Where these three ingredients have been present, the results have been impressive. Unintended pregnancies, including among the disadvantaged, have dropped, and so have Medicaid and other government expenditures. A study of the Colorado Family Planning Initiative by Sue Ricketts and her colleagues found that expanding access to LARCs decreased births to unmarried disadvantaged young women by 27 percent between 2009 and 2011. The [Contraceptive] CHOICE Project in St. Louis found that women who used LARCs or contraceptive shots had far lower rates of unintended pregnancy than users of other popular methods.

My hope is that 30 years from now this new family planning revolution will have the same degree of impact on parenting behavior, income, and children's educational achievement as the advent of the pill. My only regret is that neither Senator Moynihan nor I will be here to see whether my optimism is warranted.

> "Examining American society as a whole and the role of family life in shaping that society, a good case can be made that the main problem with helicopter parents is that there aren't nearly enough of them."

Single Parents Should Be Better Educated

Brink Lindsey

Brink Lindsey is an author and a senior fellow at the Cato Institute. In the following viewpoint, he examines research that shows that families with well-educated parents have a number of advantages. Well-educated parents make more money, are more financially stable, live in better neighborhoods, send their children to better schools, and have a more involved parenting style. Lindsey contends that this parenting style, known as helicopter parenting, is often ridiculed in the media as obsessive and annoying. However, studies show that kids reared by helicopter parents grow up with more intellectual stimulation, exhibit greater educational achievement, and become productive and highly skilled workers. Lindsey concludes that American society would benefit from more helicopter parents.

As you read, consider the following questions:

1. According to Lindsey, what percentage of children who have a parent with a bachelor's or higher degree were living with two married parents in 2011?

2. How much more does Lindsey estimate the average college graduate today makes than the average high school graduate?

3. According to child psychologists Betty Hart and Todd Risley, how many words have children of professional parents heard by the time they reach age three?

Today's hyperventilating "helicopter parents" are comic fish in a barrel. Playing Mozart to their babies in utero and dangling Baby Einstein gewgaws over their bassinets. Obsessing over peanut allergies, turning school science fairs into arms races of one-upmanship, and hiring batteries of private tutors to eke out another 10 points on the SAT [standardized test for college admission]. When we stop giggling, it's only to cluck with disapproval. Katie Roiphe, writing in *Slate*, says that overparenting "is about too much presence, but it's also about the wrong kind of presence. In fact, it can be reasonably read by children as absence, as not caring about what is really going on with them, as ignoring the specifics of them for some idealized cultural script of how they should be."

Well-educated parents of means these days do have their own distinctive way of messing things up. And so it's entirely appropriate for those of us in this group to mock and admonish ourselves into lightening up a bit. Yet when we extend our gaze beyond the relatively narrow confines of college-educated parents and their college-bound kids, things look very different.

Examining American society as a whole and the role of family life in shaping that society, a good case can be made that the main problem with helicopter parents is that there aren't nearly enough of them.

The Parenthood Divide

The kind of intensively hands-on parenting that we now like to lampoon and criticize is of relatively recent vintage. In this regard, it's worth noting that the terms "helicopter parent" and "overparenting" only entered general usage in the past decade or so. New words were needed to describe a new phenomenon. We can actually document its emergence statistically: According to husband-and-wife economists Garey and Valerie Ramey, starting in the 1990s parents began spending significantly more time with their kids.

And what really stands out in the Rameys' findings is a clear distinction between college-educated parents and everybody else. Prior to 1995, college-educated moms averaged about 12 hours a week with their kids, compared to about 11 hours for less educated moms. By 2007, though, the figure for less educated moms had risen to nearly 16 hours while that for college-educated moms had soared all the way to 21 hours. Similar trends were observed for fathers: The time that college-educated dads spent with their kids rose from 5 to 10 hours, while for less educated dads the increase was from around 4 hours to around 8 hours.

So while the time parents spend with children living at home has increased across the board, the trend has been especially pronounced among highly educated households. The parental attention gap is growing.

This is part of a larger parenting shift that breaks down along class lines. Through in-depth observation of family life in select homes, the sociologist Annette Lareau has identified clear differences in parenting across the socioeconomic spectrum. Among the poor and working-class families she studied, the focus of parenting was on what she calls "the accomplishment of natural growth." In these families, "parents viewed children's development as unfolding spontaneously, as long as they were provided with comfort, food, shelter, and other basic support."

College-educated parents have taken on a much more ambitious role—one that Lareau calls "concerted cultivation." "In these families, parents actively fostered and assessed their children's talents, opinions, and skills," Lareau writes. "They made a deliberate and sustained effort to stimulate children's development and to cultivate their cognitive and social skills."

The findings of Lareau and the Rameys document the emergence of a growing class divide in American family life. But the fissure is actually much wider than the work of these scholars shows it to be. The parenting gap isn't just about how much time parents spend with their kids. It's also about whether they live together with their kids.

The Rise of the Single-Parent Household

Over the course of the past half century, American society generally has seen a dramatic rise in single-parent families. Children born to unmarried mothers have soared from 10 percent of the total in 1969 to an astonishing 41 percent in 2008. Meanwhile, the share of children living with two married parents has fallen from 77 percent in 1980 to 65 percent in 2011.

The rise in single-parent households is much more pronounced among minority families. In 2008, 29 percent of white, non-Hispanic children were born to single mothers, compared to 53 percent of Hispanic children and 72 percent of black children. In 2011, 75 percent of white, non-Hispanic children were living with two married parents, while the same could be said for 60 percent of Hispanic children and only 33 percent of black children.

These racial cleavages are largely explained by a similar divide along class lines. As of 2011, 87 percent of children who have a parent with a bachelor's or higher degree were living with two married parents. The corresponding figures for high school grads and high school dropouts were 53 and 47 percent, respectively.

A major contributor to the growing class differences in family structure is the emergence in recent decades of a "divorce divide" along educational lines. Divorce rates have traditionally been lower for college-educated couples than for the rest of the population, but marriage breakup rates for everybody soared during the 1960s and '70s. For women whose first marriage occurred between 1970 and 1974, the share whose marriage failed within 10 years stood at 24.3 percent for those with a college degree or better and 33.7 percent for the rest. But since the '70s, divorce rates among the highly educated have fallen significantly; among non-college grads, by contrast, they have stayed high. Specifically, only 16.7 percent of women with at least a college degree experienced a marital dissolution within 10 years of a first marriage between 1990 and 1994—a 31 percent drop from 20 years earlier. For other women, though, the marriage breakup rate in the latter period was now 35.7 percent—6 percent higher than 20 years before.

Family life on either side of the class divide has thus been heading in opposite directions over the past few decades. Among the roughly 30 percent of Americans with college degrees, marriages have grown more stable and parents have committed themselves to a more intensive, hands-on, and time-consuming approach to raising children. But for everybody else, a more modest increase in time commitment by parents in intact families has been swamped by a rising tide of family breakdown. Children of the well-educated elite now receive unprecedented parental attention aimed at "concerted cultivation" of the skills they will need to thrive in today's highly complex knowledge economy. Other kids, meanwhile, are left more on their own in the traditional style—except that now the "accomplishment of natural growth" is hampered by all the distractions, disruptions, and stresses of family breakup.

The Connection with Income Inequality

It's no coincidence that rising inequality in the home has been occurring at precisely the same time as rising inequality in the workplace. These two kinds of social polarization—one cultural, the other economic—are interrelated and mutually reinforcing.

Discussions of economic inequality often focus on the top 1 percent of earners versus the other 99 percent. But the more socially significant distinction is the one between the 30 percent and the 70 percent—between, that is, the 30 percent of Americans who have college degrees and everybody else.

The average college grad today makes about 70 percent more than the average high school grad—up from around 30 percent back in 1980. According to data compiled by the Economic Policy Institute, wages for college grads rose 23 percent between 1979 and 2007 after adjusting for inflation, while real wages for workers with advanced degrees climbed by 27 percent. Meanwhile, the inflation-adjusted wages for high school grads actually fell 3 percent over the same period, and those for high school dropouts dropped by 17 percent. If you add fringe benefits to wages and make different adjustments for inflation, you can make the numbers look better for everybody, but the disparities will remain.

Why have wages for the college educated and everybody else been moving in opposite directions? It's a simple story of supply and demand: The demand for highly skilled workers has kept growing as the economy gets ever more advanced and complex, but the supply of those workers has failed to keep up. According to Harvard economists Claudia Goldin and Lawrence Katz, the relative supply of college graduates rose at an average rate of only 2 percent a year between 1980 and 2005—a steep decline from the average rate of 3.8 percent a year that prevailed between 1960 and 1980. And all of the growth that has occurred has been due to women: The college graduation rate for young men is roughly the same as it was in 1980.

Things would surely look very different if the trends in college-educated homes toward greater family stability and "concerted cultivation" had been mirrored in the rest of the country. Consider, for example, a recent study by economists Sheldon Danziger and Patrick Wightman. Looking back at people born between 1956 and 1958, they found that 37 percent of those born to college-educated parents could expect to finish college by age 25, compared to only 8 percent of those whose parents had a high school education or less. Fast-forward to people born between 1979 and 1982, and the share of the kids of college-educated parents who earned a college degree by 25 had risen to 53 percent, while for the kids of high school grads and dropouts the share had slipped to 6 percent.

In other words, families with well-educated parents have been moving in sync with economic trends: They have been increasingly likely to produce new college grads in step with the rising demand for highly skilled workers. For families with less educated parents, however, there has been a total disconnect. And as a result, their kids have been falling behind.

More Helicopter Parents, Please

The advantages of having well-educated parents are varied. Smart parents who naturally do well in school pass on their genes. They also tend to make more money, which can buy a safer neighborhood and a higher quality education. But a less appreciated advantage is that college-educated parents are more likely to dote obsessively—even, yes, comically—on their children. And there is evidence that the very nature of their parenting style is good for grooming productive workers.

Thanks to Malcolm Gladwell's best-selling *Outliers*, many of us are now familiar with the "10,000 hour rule": In almost any field you can think of, you can't perform at the very highest level without logging the requisite hours of diligent, focused practice. The move in well-educated homes toward "concerted cultivation"—or helicopter parenting, if we want to be snarky about its sometimes absurd excesses—can be seen as an effort to inject a lot more deliberate practice into childhood. Practice, in particular, at developing the skills needed to excel in school, and later in the workplace.

Most obviously, the children of well-educated parents receive much more intellectual stimulation in the home than do other kids. For example, child psychologists Betty Hart and Todd Risley estimate that by the time they reach age three, children of professional parents have heard some 45 million words addressed to them—as opposed to only 26 million words for working-class kids, and a mere 13 million words in the case of kids on welfare. By the time kids start school, kids of well-educated parents are much better prepared than their classmates. Consequently, they're much more likely to receive praise and encouragement from their teachers, which means their attitudes about being in school are much more likely to be positive. Even relatively small advantages conferred early in life can thus snowball over time.

The deliberate practice that is going on constantly in well-educated homes extends beyond purely intellectual pursuits. As they march their kids through the weekly gauntlet of organized activities, the practitioners of concerted cultivation are drilling their kids in a host of skills critical to academic and economic success. Skills like managing one's time by making and keeping schedules, getting along with other people from different backgrounds on the basis of common interests, and deferring gratification in order to maximize rewards down the road. All of these, as well as fluency in the three Rs [reading, writing, and arithmetic (math)], are vital components of "human capital"—economist-speak for economically valuable skills.

So by all means, keep making fun of helicopter parents. The delusion that drives them off the deep end—that, with enough exertion and planning, the crooked timber of their little ones can be lathed to perfection—is, after all, risible. But keep in mind that the excesses of concerted cultivation are of little account when compared to the deficits that now afflict so many homes. Those deficits are a major factor behind some of the thorniest problems in American society today, from multigenerational poverty and mediocre and worse schools to stagnant wages for large segments of the workforce. Policy makers tasked with addressing these problems face the daunting challenge of designing bureaucratic substitutes for the hovering, loving harassment supplied by Mom and Dad. A tall order, indeed.

> *"If lengthy mandatory minimum sen-*
> *tences for nonviolent drug addicts actu-*
> *ally worked, one might be able to ra-*
> *tionalize them. But there is no evidence*
> *that they do."*

How Mandatory Minimums Forced Me to Send More than 1,000 Nonviolent Drug Offenders to Federal Prison

Mark W. Bennett

Mark W. Bennett is a federal judge. In the following viewpoint, he reflects on his experience on the bench, focusing on the large numbers of men and women he has sentenced to federal prisons for nonviolent drug charges because of mandatory minimum sentences. These mandatory minimums take away judicial discretion in sentencing, dictating the minimum number of years a convicted offender can be given in jail. Bennett observes that there is no evidence that mandatory minimum sentences work; in fact, they largely function to take parents away from their children for long periods of time for minor nonviolent drug charges. Although it is unorthodox for federal judges to comment on such matters, Bennett feels compelled to speak out in favor of sentencing reform out of public concern and a broader sense of fairness and compassion.

As you read, consider the following questions:

1. According to Bennett, how many Americans has he sent to federal prison for mandatory minimum sentences ranging from sixty months to life without the possibility of release?

2. According to the viewpoint, how many district courts are there across the United States?

3. According to a 2010 survey of federal district court judges, what percentage said mandatory minimum sentences were too harsh?

Growing up in blue-collar Circle Pines, Minnesota, in the 1950s, raised by parents from the "Greatest Generation," I dreamed only of becoming a civil rights lawyer. My passion for justice was hardwired into my DNA. Never could I have imagined that by the end of my 50s, after nineteen years as one of 678 federal district court judges in the nation, I would have sent 1,092 of my fellow citizens to federal prison for mandatory minimum sentences ranging from sixty months to life without the possibility of release. The majority of these women, men and young adults are nonviolent drug addicts. Methamphetamine is their drug of choice. Crack cocaine is a distant second. Drug kingpins? Oh yes, I've sentenced them, too. But I can count them on one hand. While I'm extremely proud of my father's service in World War II, I am greatly conflicted about my role in the "war on drugs."

The Role of Drugs

You might think the Northern District of Iowa—a bucolic area home to just one city with a population above 100,000—is a sleepy place with few federal crimes. You would be wrong.

Of the ninety-four district courts across the United States, we have the sixth-heaviest criminal caseload per judge. Here in the heartland, I sentence more drug offenders in a single year than the average federal district court judge in New York City, Washington, Chicago, Minneapolis and San Francisco—*combined*. While drug cases nationally make up 29 percent of federal judges' criminal dockets, according to the US Sentencing Commission, they make up more than 56 percent of mine. More startling, while meth cases make up 18 percent of a judge's drug docket nationally, they account for 78 percent of mine. Add crack cocaine and together they account for 87 percent.

Crack defendants are almost always poor African Americans. Meth defendants are generally lower-income whites. More than 80 percent of the 4,546 meth defendants sentenced in federal courts in 2010 received a mandatory minimum sentence. These small-time addicts are apprehended not through high-tech wiretaps or sophisticated undercover stings but by common traffic stops for things like nonfunctioning taillights. Or they're caught in a search of the logs at a local Walmart to see who is buying unusually large amounts of nonprescription cold medicine. They are the low-hanging fruit of the drug war. Other than their crippling meth addiction, they are very much like the folks I grew up with. Virtually all are charged with federal drug trafficking conspiracy—which sounds ominous but is based on something as simple as two people agreeing to purchase pseudoephedrine and cook it into meth. They don't even have to succeed.

I recently sentenced a group of more than twenty defendants on meth trafficking conspiracy charges. All of them pled guilty. Eighteen were "pill smurfers," as federal prosecutors put it, meaning their role amounted to regularly buying and delivering cold medicine to meth cookers in exchange for very small, low-grade quantities to feed their severe addictions. Most were unemployed or underemployed. Several were single mothers. They did not sell or directly distribute meth; there were no hoards of cash, guns or countersurveillance equipment. Yet all of them faced mandatory minimum sentences of sixty or 120 months. One meth-addicted mother faced a 240-month sentence because a prior meth conviction in county court doubled her mandatory minimum. She will likely serve all twenty years; in the federal system, there is no parole, and one serves an entire sentence minus a maximum of a 15 percent reduction rewarded for "good time."

The Need for Sentencing Reform

Several years ago, I started visiting inmates I had sentenced in prison. It is deeply inspiring to see the positive changes most have made. Some definitely needed the wake-up call of a prison cell, but very few need more than two or three years behind bars. These men and women need intensive drug treatment, and most of the inmates I visit are working hard to turn their lives around. They are shocked—and glad—to see me, and it's important to them that people outside prison care about their progress. For far too many, I am their only visitor.

If lengthy mandatory minimum sentences for nonviolent drug addicts actually worked, one might be able to rationalize them. But there is no evidence that they do. I have seen how they leave hundreds of thousands of young children parentless and thousands of aging, infirm and dying parents childless. They destroy families and mightily fuel the cycle of poverty and addiction. In fact, I have been at this so long, I am now sentencing the grown children of people I long ago sent to prison.

For years I have debriefed jurors after their verdicts. Northwest Iowa is one of the most conservative regions in the country, and these are people who, for the most part, think judges are too soft on crime. Yet, for all the times I've asked jurors after a drug conviction what they think a fair sentence would

America and Its Incarceration Problem

As a nation, we are coldly efficient in our incarceration efforts. While the entire U.S. population has increased by about a third since 1980, the federal prison population has grown at an astonishing rate—by almost 800 percent. It's still growing—despite the fact that federal prisons are operating at nearly 40 percent above capacity. Even though this country comprises just 5 percent of the world's population, we incarcerate almost a quarter of the world's prisoners. More than 219,000 federal inmates are currently behind bars. Almost half of them are serving time for drug-related crimes, and many have substance use disorders. Nine to 10 million more people cycle through America's local jails each year. And roughly 40 percent of former federal prisoners—and more than 60 percent of former state prisoners—are rearrested or have their supervision revoked within three years after their release, at great cost to American taxpayers and often for technical or minor violations of the terms of their release.

Attorney General Eric Holder,
Speech to the Annual Meeting of the American Bar
Association's House of Delegates, August 12, 2013.

be, never has one given a figure even close to the mandatory minimum. It is always far lower. Like people who dislike Congress but like their Congress member, these jurors think the criminal justice system coddles criminals in the abstract—but when confronted by a real live defendant, even a "drug trafficker," they never find a mandatory minimum sentence to be a just sentence.

Many people across the political spectrum have spoken out against the insanity of mandatory minimums. These include our past three presidents, as well as Supreme Court justices William Rehnquist, whom nobody could dismiss as "soft on crime," and Anthony Kennedy, who told the American Bar Association in 2003, "I can accept neither the necessity nor the wisdom of federal mandatory minimum sentences." In 2005, four former attorneys general, a former FBI [Federal Bureau of Investigation] director and dozens of former federal prosecutors, judges and Justice Department officials filed an amicus brief in the Supreme Court opposing the use of mandatory minimums in a case involving a marijuana defendant facing a fifty-five-year sentence. In 2008, the *Christian Science Monitor* reported that 60 percent of Americans opposed mandatory minimums for nonviolent offenders. And in a 2010 survey of federal district court judges, 62 percent said mandatory minimums were too harsh.

Federal judges have a long-standing culture of not speaking out on issues of public concern. I am breaking with this tradition not because I am eager to but because the daily grist of what I do compels me to. In 1999, Judge Robert Pratt of the Southern District of Iowa, a courageous jurist whose brilliant opinion in *Gall v. United States* led to one of the most important Supreme Court sentencing opinions in my professional life, wrote a guest editorial in the *Des Moines Register* criticizing federal sentencing guidelines and mandatory minimums. He ended by asking, "If we don't speak up, who will?" I hope more of my colleagues will speak up, regardless of their position on the fairness of mandatory minimum sentences for nonviolent drug offenders. This is an issue of grave national consequence. Might there be a problem when the United States of America incarcerates a higher percentage of its population than any nation in the world?

> *"The way in which these [immigration] policies are being carried out is destroying the fabric of immigrant communities across the nation."*

Immigration Reform Would Benefit Many Single-Parent Families

Clarissa Martinez-De-Castro

Clarissa Martinez-De-Castro is the director of Immigration and Civic Engagement for the National Council of La Raza. In the following viewpoint, she urges the US Congress to pass immigration reform legislation that would address the country's broken immigration system. In recent years, there has been an increase in deportations that has functioned to break up families, increase levels of social and economic instability, and devastate communities. Martinez-De-Castro advocates for reform that will provide a path to citizenship, reunite many of these broken families, and strengthen the existing family immigration system. This reform would also have to include same-sex couples. Martinez-De-Castro says that America's immigration system needs to be forward-thinking and flexible enough to meet today's realities and address the challenges of a changing economy.

Clarissa Martinez-De-Castro, "Strong Families: An Economic and Social Imperative for Successful Immigration Reform," March 14, 2013. Judiciary.House.gov. Courtesy of the Subcommittee on Immigration and Border Security/United States House of Representatives.

As you read, consider the following questions:

1. According to the author, how many parents of US citizens were deported between July 1, 2010, and September 31, 2012?

2. How many undocumented immigrants have lived in the United States for a decade or more, according to Martinez-De-Castro?

3. What does the author view as a key missing aspect of the 1986 immigration reform law?

Despite the many compelling reasons for ensuring that families are united, our current immigration system separates mixed-status families—that is, families made up of U.S. citizens or legal permanent residents (LPRs) who are the spouses, children, parents, and siblings of undocumented immigrants.

The rapid increase in deportations over the last four years is having a devastating effect on families. Our deportation policies literally destroy families and force U.S. citizens into public assistance, foster care, or exile from the United States. Hundreds of thousands of U.S. citizens and lawful permanent residents have been separated from family members. For example, between July 1, 2010, and September 31, 2012, the Department of Homeland Security (DHS) deported 204,810 parents of U.S. citizens.

In mixed-status families, many have tried to adjust their immigration status, and have spent fortunes in immigration fees and lawyers' fees, but have failed. As one U.S. citizen married to an undocumented immigrant stated, "People who don't have undocumented family members don't believe me when I tell them he can't get papers." It is commonly believed that if a U.S. citizen marries an immigrant, the foreign-born spouse is quickly or even instantly granted U.S. citizenship. The reality is that for most people who entered without a visa, or who overstayed a visa, it is very difficult and often impossible to obtain legal status. Anyone who has been in the U.S. for more than six months out of legal status is barred from reentry for three years, and those who have been out of status for one year or more are barred from reentering for ten years, due to provisions in the Illegal Immigration Reform and Immigrant Responsibility Act of 1996 (IIRIRA).

So when you hear on talk radio, "Why don't these people go out and come back the right way?," the answer is that, because of IIRIRA, we have created an incredible disincentive for those with legal claims to adjust their status, to get legal, because they would face exile from their families, and therefore push them to remain in the undocumented underground.

A Catch-22

This puts many families who seek to adjust the status of their loved one through legal channels in a terrible catch-22. They must leave the United States in order to apply for an immigrant visa at a U.S. consulate, but once they depart the U.S. for that visa, they may be barred from reentering for as long as ten years. At NCLR [National Council of La Raza], we know of countless stories of U.S. citizens and permanent residents who are separated from their spouses because of the three- and ten-year bars to reentry. For many of these spouses, they never imagined that by trying to follow the rule of law their family would be ripped apart.

Take the case of Elizabeth, an American citizen from Cleveland, Ohio. Elizabeth served in the National Guard and the Marine Corps. She served in Afghanistan during Operation Enduring Freedom. After she left the Marines, Elizabeth fell in love and married Marcos. The very same day Elizabeth and Marcos celebrated the news that they had a second child on the way, Marcos was stopped on his way to work. Marcos was undocumented. He was deported a month later. Elizabeth was left behind, without the family's breadwinner, pregnant and

Immigration Controversy

In a majority of Western countries, the issue of contemporary immigration tends to be highly emotive. In very few countries, including states like Israel and Australia, which remain huge net importers of immigrants, do the famous sentiments expressed on the Statue of Liberty ("Give me your tired, your poor, your huddled masses yearning to breathe free . . .") still ring true. Immigration is frequently a response to a hard-faced economic need. Many immigrants, seeking a better life for future generations of their family, arrive in industrialized nations prepared to fulfill laborious, dirty, and unskilled but necessary jobs that few in the native population will undertake. The immigrants still face hostility and xenophobia in the new nation. Indeed, large segments of the population in some industrialized countries are so opposed to allowing more immigrants into their borders that immigration—whether legal or illegal—has become a defining electoral issue.

"Immigrants and Immigration,"
Gale Global Issues in Context, *2015.*

with a small child. That was three years ago. She is someone who takes pride in following the rules, in going through the system and following available processes. She has done exhaustive research and gotten legal assistance. As she tells it, "we want to do it the right way, but every door has been slammed in our face." Marcos has been declined a consular interview until 2020. Elizabeth has even considered moving to Mexico, so the children can be with both mom and dad, but this is her country. She is fighting to keep her family afloat, bring it back together. She traveled to DC last week and walked the halls of Congress, for the first time ever, with many other family members that share similarly devastating stories.

This forced separation of families has increased exponentially as a result of current enforcement policies. By nearly every standard, more is being done than ever before to enforce immigration laws. Measured in terms of dollars, not only are we spending more on immigration enforcement than at any time in history, but the federal government today spends more on enforcing immigration laws than on all other categories of federal law enforcement combined. Measured in qualitative terms, never before has our country used a broader array of enforcement strategies than we do today.

The way in which these policies are being carried out is destroying the fabric of immigrant communities across the nation. And the magnitude of that devastation goes beyond immigrant communities, as the lives and fate of immigrants are fundamentally interwoven with those of citizens, as Elizabeth's story illustrates. Most undocumented immigrants are long-term U.S. residents; two-thirds have lived here for a decade or more. They work hard, pay taxes, and otherwise abide by our laws. They provide for U.S. citizen spouses and children; they are our fellow churchgoers and children's playmates. Some of them came to this country as children, and this is the only country they know and consider home. The interests of our country are best served by allowing these long-term residents to come forward, pass a background check, pay taxes, learn English, and earn the ability to apply for citizenship just like every other group of immigrants before them. An immigration bill must not create a permanent subclass of individuals who are expected to support the rest of us in our pursuit of the American dream without having access to it themselves.

The Solution

Our visa policies have to conform with reality, so that in ten years' time, we are not back here talking about legalizing another population of undocumented immigrants who, like those today, had no option to come in legally, and came illegally instead. This is the key difference between the immigration debate in 2013 and the immigration debate in 1986. Back then, we legalized a portion of the undocumented, myself included, and put in place a new regime of workplace enforcement that did not on its own curtail illegal immigration. A key missing aspect of the 1986 legislation is that it did not fix the underlying legal immigration system, resulting in a continuing mismatch between the supply of immigration visas and the demand for legal immigration as determined by families and our vibrant economy. You have a chance to do it right this time, and the decisions you make in the coming weeks and months are very important. In order for our visa policies to comport with and effectively regulate reality, they have to be both generous and flexible.

We know from the history of people coming to this country that some people will come for jobs, intending to go home someday. Some people will come with their families, intending to make this their permanent new home. Some who come permanently will decide to leave. Some who come temporarily will decide to stay. And factors like love, families, children, and careers, inevitably make matters complex. We have to have an immigration system in the 21st century that reflects those complexities and includes channels that address a mix of permanent and temporary, of family and business, of education and marriage channels, and that does not lock individuals out of legal status or citizenship, if they play by the rules.

Adhering to American Values

NCLR supports employment-based immigration because done right it can help strengthen our economy. But we must be careful not to pursue improvements in this area by undermining family immigration or denying the powerful role the latter plays in the social and economic integration of immigrants in our country. Let's remember the principles that should guide us—to restore the rule of law, preserve the rule of law, and strengthen the fabric of America. This can only be accomplished with a functioning family immigration system, working in complement with our employment-based immigration system.

I would urge this subcommittee [the House Subcommittee on Immigration and Border Security] to think in terms of both/and rather than either/or. Undue restrictions on employment-based legal immigration have the potential to rob the American economy of talent that can create jobs and improve our national well-being and could lead to unintended consequences, like offshoring of jobs or incentives to work around the limits of our legal immigration system. But you must also realize that undue restrictions on family immigration have the exact same potential, in addition to keeping families separated, or encouraging them to break the law because they have no other choice, and slowing the integration and success of immigrants in our country.

For example, creating a visa program for graduates in science, technology, engineering and math (STEM) fields is a good idea that both parties embrace. But if we are reducing other legal immigration channels in order to create a new one, we are forcing ourselves into a trap, a false choice. We are not for unlimited immigration, we are not for open borders, we are not for immigration on demand. But as with any sensible regulation of an aspect of the American economy, that regulatory regime has to be based in reality and responsive to the market forces of supply and demand. If we are going to end illegal immigration, which should be our shared goal, then we must have a flexible, dynamic, and multipronged legal immigration system that creates incentives to follow the rules rather than incentives to go around the system.

We should also realize that in 2013, many states and many countries recognize the reality that some couples, some families, and some long-term committed relationships involve same-sex couples. If our immigration laws exclude same-sex couples, we are forcing people who can contribute to our country to leave or creating incentives for reunification outside our legal system rather than within the structure of sensible laws.

My husband's great-grandfather came from Russia as part of a family unit in the 1880s. Another great-grandfather came as a young man from Canada seeking business opportunities. My parents came in the early [19]80s, but eventually went back. I stayed, was able to get an education, became a citizen, married, and have made my life here. My family and my husband's family include PhDs, factory workers, and office workers; gay and straight people; different religious denominations and political orientations—just like every other American family. We need a legal immigration system as varied and colorful as my modern family, in order to do the job of regulating immigration in 21st-century America. [It] is a huge challenge, but failure is not an option.

"I don't think a country as great as ours should pay people so little that they need help from the state just to survive."

A Minimum-Wage Hike Would Help Single-Parent Families

Thomas E. Perez

Thomas E. Perez is the secretary of the US Department of Labor. In the following viewpoint, he testifies that an increase in the minimum wage is essential to America's long-term economic health. Perez argues that raising the minimum wage from the current level of $7.25 per hour to $10.10 per hour will provide hardworking Americans with a living wage and result in greater economic security for families. Many of those who would benefit are single mothers who are trying to raise families on minimum-wage jobs. Many businesses are also in favor of a minimum-wage hike because it leads to happier, more experienced employees. A number of states already have passed laws to raise the minimum wage, but legislation is needed on the federal level. Perez encourages the US Congress to act on minimum-wage legislation to support the American worker.

Thomas E. Perez, "Testimony Before the Health, Education, Labor and Pensions Committee," March 12, 2014. Help.Senate.gov. Courtesy of the US Senate Committee on Health Education, Labor and Pensions.

As you read, consider the following questions:

1. According to the Council of Economic Advisers (CEA), how many American workers would benefit from a minimum-wage increase?

2. How long has the minimum wage been frozen at $7.25 per hour?

3. According to a Small Business Majority poll, what percentage of entrepreneurs support raising the minimum wage to $10.10 per hour?

In his State of the Union address, President [Barack] Obama laid out an agenda based on the principle of opportunity for all. What's always set America apart is the belief that our destinies shouldn't be predetermined by the circumstances of our birth. Everyone, through hard work and personal responsibility, should have the chance to succeed and create a better life for themselves and their families.

To realize that vision, we have to continue to grow the economy and the availability of jobs with good wages—jobs in construction, in manufacturing, in energy and throughout the economy. We also need to provide training opportunities to empower our workers with the skills and credentials that enable them to get those jobs—that is, in fact, one of the linchpins of our work at the U.S. Department of Labor. It all has to start with a world-class education, beginning when a child is four years old. It includes access to affordable health care that is always there when you need it. And it includes the opportunity to build a nest egg and save for retirement.

This vision is embedded in the American social contract. It is consistent with the idea that we don't leave anyone behind. That, when times are tough, Americans don't say everyone is on their own to fend for themselves. We say that we're all in this together.

The Minimum Wage

And at the heart of it all is the belief that hard work must pay off, that Americans deserve a wage they can live on. That is why President Obama believes we must raise the federal minimum wage from the current level of $7.25 to $10.10 per hour. Many members of this committee [the Senate Committee on Health, Education, Labor, and Pensions] have been strong supporters of this increase; but none more so than Chairman [Tom] Harkin, as the sponsor of S. 460 [a bill to increase the minimum wage] and a relentless champion for working families throughout nearly four decades of service in the House and the Senate.

Americans deserve a raise. Increasing the federal minimum wage to $10.10 would make a powerful difference in millions of lives. Based on tabulations from the Council of Economic Advisers (CEA), it would benefit 28 million workers, giving them a little bit more breathing room and peace of mind. It would raise incomes for an estimated 12 million people now in poverty, lifting about 2 million of them out of poverty.

The federal minimum wage has been frozen at $7.25 an hour since 2009. Meanwhile, the price of almost everything a working family needs to live their lives is going up. A gallon of milk, a gallon of gas, a month's rent, a pair of children's shoes—of course, they all cost more than they did in 2009. In fact, the purchasing power of the minimum wage has been on a steady decline for many decades. It's worth about 20 percent less than it was when President [Ronald] Reagan took office. Adjusting for inflation, the minimum wage peaked in the 1960s at $10.69 in today's dollars, 47 percent *more* than its current value.

That diminishing value is undermining the economic security of millions of families. It has contributed to deepening inequality and a lack of upward mobility throughout the country, because, despite the myth that's been propagated, minimum-wage workers are not just teenagers looking to earn a little extra to supplement their allowances. In fact, according to CEA, 88 percent of those who would benefit from an increase to $10.10 an hour are age 20 or over and more than 50 percent are women, many of whom have children.

Why do we expect her to take home less even though she's producing more? According to data from the Bureau of Labor Statistics (BLS), since 1979, worker productivity has increased more than 90 percent but real average hourly earnings of production and non-supervisory workers have barely budged—up only 1.3 percent.

The Challenge of Today's Minimum Wage

I've visited with these hardworking Americans and heard their stories, heartbreaking stories about what it's like to live at or near the minimum wage: The wrenching decisions you have to make. The daily grind and struggle. The apprehension and anxiety. The exhaustion and sense of futility. But these are also people with immense pride, dignity and self-respect. They don't want a handout; they just want a fair day's pay for a fair day's work.

I met with one woman from Durham, North Carolina, who, despite 16 years working in the fast-food industry, can't even afford a place of her own. She's staying with her adult children and can barely afford the life-sustaining medicine she needs. "We work hard," she told me. "We just want to be treated fair. We want to help ourselves." She knows what it's like to go without. "It's a sad day in America," she said, when you can feed your kids but you can't eat yourself.

In Louisville, I talked with a woman named Honey Dozier who is trying to raise four children on the $7.25 an hour she earns working concessions at a bowling alley. As she put it: "I feel like I have to choose either providing food and necessities for my family or health care, because I can't afford both this month." She also expressed sorrow at the fact that "when you work a low-paying job, you don't earn enough to be a good mother. I don't mind giving 100 percent to my employer, but I should also give 100 percent to my family, and a $7.25 wage doesn't allow that."

Another man from New York talked about having his gas and electricity cut off for two months. He told me: "My mom recently got laid off . . . we had an eviction notice . . . and my mom took out a loan, which I don't think she can pay back."

One St. Louis man is trying hard to climb into the middle class but as he described it: "I'm working 70 hours a week . . . my day starts at 6 A.M. . . . I want to go to college, [but] I don't have time [and] I can't afford it." He added: "I shouldn't have to decide: Am I going to pay the electric bill or do I pay the heat? I'm a thousand dollars behind in rent now . . . where is this money going to come from?" He has goals and ambition—we ought to ensure that he has the opportunity to make the most of his abilities and live out his dreams.

He also added that he has burn marks on his arm from working in a commercial kitchen. He can't afford to take a day off from work, even when he has the flu. And this is someone who handles food for a living.

America Must Do Better

It's startling to learn just how many of these workers are forced to go on food stamps and other forms of public assistance just to make ends meet. A recent study from the University of California, Berkeley concluded that workers in the fast-food industry are relying on safety net programs to the tune of a staggering $7 billion a year. A young fast-food worker from Milwaukee understands the implications. All that money in public assistance, he explained, "could be used on something else to better the community," if only businesses paid higher than poverty wages.

Not every low-wage worker is in the food services industry, however. From farmworkers to motion picture projectionists, there are people struggling at or near the minimum wage. If you work in ski patrol or in the gaming industry or in animal care, you stand to gain from an increase in the minimum wage. Even jobs we associate with a white-collar environment, like bank tellers, are struggling at the very bottom of the wage scale. According to an analysis by a group called the Committee for Better Banks, one-third of bank tellers are depending on government programs to get by—$105 million in food stamps, $250 million through the earned income tax credit, and $534 million in Medicaid and the Children's Health Insurance Program each year.

I think we're better than this. I don't think a country as great as ours should pay people so little that they need help from the state just to survive. What that amounts to is billions of dollars in taxpayer subsidies for very profitable companies. The American people are filling the gap and stepping in for employers who refuse to pay a wage that their workers can survive on. A recent study from the Center for American Progress concluded that if the [Tom] Harkin–[George] Miller legislation [minimum wage hike] becomes law, it would mean as many as 3.8 million fewer people enrolled in the Supplemental Nutrition Assistance Program (SNAP), thus reducing spending by nearly $4.6 billion a year.

The Influence of U.S. Business

But it's not just workers themselves who are making the case for a higher minimum wage. Contrary to the conventional wisdom, businesses of all sizes are increasingly embracing the idea too. I've met with them as well, and it's clear that they want to do right by their employees, that they want to take the high road, that they aren't interested in running a race to the bottom. In fact, just last week [in March 2014] Small Business Majority released the findings of a new poll demonstrating that 57 percent of entrepreneurs support raising the minimum wage to $10.10 per hour.

The morning after the State of the Union, I joined the president on a visit to a Costco store just down the road in Prince George's County Maryland. Costco has built a wildly successful business based on the idea that you can pay good wages while selling quality products at affordable prices. They've rejected the false choice that says you can serve the interests of your shareholders, or you can serve the interests of your employees, but not both.

I saw the same approach the next day on a visit to an Ace Hardware store just a few blocks away from here. Most of the employees there make $10 per hour. The owner, Gina Schaefer, talks about how a better wage sends the message that "we value our employees . . . as assets to the business because we know they are the people who are on the front lines with our customers." Better-paid employees are also longer-serving employees, she explained. That translates into "robust knowledge of the products we sell and the services we provide," which means the kind of excellent customer service that has helped Gina build, in just over a decade, a thriving business of nine stores employing 185 people.

A Successful Business Model

But she's not an outlier or an aberration. I talk to employers large and small who understand that raising wages is in their own self-interest and part of a successful business model. It keeps employees loyal and productive. It increases morale and reduces absenteeism.

I spoke to a group of restaurant owners recently and what I heard from them over and over again is that training costs as a result of high turnover rates are one of their biggest business expenses. One of them, a bistro owner from Brooklyn, told me he used to lose dishwashers every few months, back when he paid them $8.59 per hour. Once he bumped their pay to $11 per hour, he's had great success retaining them—he had the same four dishwashers for all of 2013, which is a pretty big deal when you're running a restaurant.

Many of the restaurant owners I met also feel strongly that we have to do something about the paltry minimum cash wage for tipped workers, which hasn't increased in more than 20 years. The law allows the employer to pay an unconscionable rate of just $2.13 per hour, and to use tips to meet the full minimum wage. Every time in recent history that the minimum wage has been debated, it seems, the interests of tipped workers get left on the cutting room floor.

They work exceedingly hard, under great pressure, at irregular hours. But according to a 2012 study by the National Employment Law Project, restaurant servers—70% of whom are women—are three times more likely to be below the poverty line than the overall workforce and twice as likely to be on food stamps. As the report puts it: "Essentially, many of the workers who serve America its food cannot afford to eat." That's why it's so vitally important that the Harkin-Miller legislation raises the minimum cash wage for tipped workers to 70 percent of the full minimum wage.

Businesses cite a lot of reasons for paying well. One gentleman who runs a record store in St. Louis talked to me about it in terms of an investment in his neighborhood: "If you think about having a relationship with your community and a relationship with your customers, it starts with your relationship to your employees."

They also very much like the idea of indexing the minimum wage to inflation over time, as the Harkin-Miller bill does. That kind of certainty and predictability is what they need to run their businesses effectively.

What I heard over and over again was the ways that higher wages provide a shot in the arm to the economy by boosting consumer demand. One man who owns a small wholesale nursery in Maryland explained that his workers "are spending 100 percent of their take home pay in the local economy. It's

recirculating. They're spending it on rent, groceries, cars, new tires—all the things you need to live."

Workers also understand the larger economic impact. The fast-food worker from Durham I met said: "If they would pay us what we need, we could put money back into the economy and pay for what we need. And that strengthens all of us."

Ask Henry Ford

This isn't a new or original idea. And no less of a capitalist than Henry Ford understood it. Exactly one hundred years ago, faced with high attrition rates that were damaging his business, he took the unusual step of doubling the wages of his assembly line workers. Because he believed that would reverberate throughout the economy. Here's how he explained his decision:

> "If we can distribute high wages, then that money is going to be spent and it will serve to make storekeepers and distributors and manufacturers and workers in other lines more

prosperous and their prosperity will be reflected in our sales. Countrywide high wages spell countrywide prosperity."

Henry Ford was as cunning a businessman as there has ever been. He believed higher wages were key to the nation's economic vitality. It's as true now as it was then—raising the minimum wage isn't just pro-worker; it's also pro-business. It isn't just the right thing to do; it's the smart thing to do.

The minimum wage is now 75 years old, having been established with President [Franklin D.] Roosevelt's signing of the Fair Labor Standards Act in 1938. And for as long as a wage floor has even been under consideration, it has been opposed by those who have claimed it would cripple the national economy.

Debunking the Myths

We hear the argument that the consumers will bear the cost of a higher minimum wage, as it will lead to higher prices, particularly on food. But a recent study by the Food Chain Workers Alliance and its partners debunks that myth. It concludes that American households, between eating in and eating out, will spend all of 10 cents more a day on food—*just 10 cents*—if the Miller-Harkin legislation becomes law.

All of the naysaying reminds me a little bit of when I served on the Montgomery County council, and we wrestled with the issue of a smoking ban in local restaurants. There was a lot of dramatic testimony about how no one would eat out anymore and it would be the ruin of the local food and beverage industry. Well, we passed the smoking ban, and I can assure you that the Montgomery County restaurants continue to do quite well.

When it comes to the minimum wage, the doomsday scenarios have never come to pass and the opponents have consistently been on the wrong side of history. The sky did not fall because we guaranteed workers a minimum level of basic economic security. The U.S. economy has continued to grow—and businesses have continued to thrive—even as the minimum wage has gone up 22 times over the last three-quarters of a century. In fact, an analysis of 64 studies of minimum-wage increases found "no evidence of a meaningful negative impact on job creation."

A Bipartisan Effort

Both Democratic and Republican lawmakers throughout the last several decades have understood this. Raising the minimum wage has historically been a bipartisan exercise, often without great contentiousness or controversy.

President George H.W. Bush and a Democratic Congress did it in 1989. President [Bill] Clinton and a Republican Congress did it in 1996. President George W. Bush and a Democratic Congress did it again in 2007. There's no reason to believe we can't and shouldn't do it in 2014.

Momentum is gathering in favor of a higher minimum wage, and it is coming from the grassroots. Throughout the country, broad coalitions are coming together to raise state and local minimum wages, either through legislative action or ballot measure. On the first of the year, in fact, an increase went into effect in 13 different states. Twenty-two states and the District of Columbia all have passed a minimum wage higher than the federal level—from Vermont to Colorado, from Connecticut to Alaska, from Massachusetts to Washington State.

Also, 24 states and the District of Columbia already have a higher cash wage for tipped workers than the federal level. Another seven states require tipped employees receive the full state minimum wage. For example, California and Oregon, both with quite successful restaurant industries, give their tipped workers full state minimum wage.

The game has changed and the ground has shifted. A sense of urgency has begun to set in. Part of that is because workers are standing up for themselves. Fast-food workers in particular have been speaking out and taking action, demanding that their hard work be rewarded with a fair wage. And their voices are resonating. More than three-quarters of the American people believe we should increase the minimum wage, according to a recent Gallup poll.

The president is doing everything he can under his authority to respond to that surge, making sure our federal procurement process reflects that emerging consensus. Last month, he made good on his State of the Union promise to sign an executive order mandating that federal contractors pay their federally funded employees working on new and replacement federal service, construction, and concession contracts at least $10.10 an hour. As he put it: "If you cook our troops' meals or wash their dishes, you shouldn't have to live in poverty."

Congress Must Act

The only thing left is for action to come from these halls. The Congress is lagging behind the states, behind public opinion, behind workers who want more opportunity, behind forward-looking business leaders who want to do well by doing good. Even the Conservative Party in Great Britain recently embraced a higher minimum wage across the Atlantic.

It is time for the Congress to lead on this urgent issue of economic security and fundamental fairness. It's time for the Congress to say that yes, it will give America a raise.

Thanks to the grit and resilience of the American people, we've come a long way toward our goal of being an opportunity society, a place where anyone can make it if they try, a place where everyone has a fair shot at getting ahead.

I am very optimistic about the direction of our economy. We've gradually emerged from the worst economic crisis of our lifetimes, and now, according to BLS, the private sector has created more than 8.7 million jobs over the last 48 months.

The manufacturing sector is resurgent. The housing market has rebounded. We've made strong investments in our citizens and their potential even as we've cut our deficits by more than half.

But too many Americans aren't experiencing this recovery or sharing in this prosperity. They are working harder and harder but falling further and further behind. They are falling short of their dreams through no fault of their own. They are finding the rungs on the ladder of opportunity beyond their reach.

Living Up to American Values

People who work full-time in the wealthiest nation on earth should not live in poverty. That is, in my view, a fundamental article of faith in our country. And yet, that's exactly what our current law mandates, with a full-time minimum wage worker earning an annual income of $14,500 a year.

That's not what a country built on opportunity does. That's no way to honor the dignity of work, or to build an economy powered by a thriving middle class. When hard-working Americans are undervalued and underpaid, then the American social contract is being breached and we are not truly living up to our values.

But when hard work and responsibility are rewarded, when every American working full-time is able to provide for their family, it makes the whole nation stronger. The Congress has the power to do that, by taking the long-overdue step of increasing the minimum wage.

The time has come to give the American people a raise. It's a raise they need, a raise they've earned, a raise they deserve. The president and I stand ready to work with you in any way on this important matter. Thank you very much, and I look forward to taking your questions.

> *"While it may sound appealing to double the pay of fast-food workers and other entry-level workers with one wave of the government's mandate wand, there's a big difference between good intentions and good results."*

A Minimum-Wage Hike Would Not Benefit Single-Parent Families

Chantal Lovell

Chantal Lovell is deputy communications director at the Nevada Policy Research Institute. In the following viewpoint, she maintains that the minimum wage should not be raised because it would kill jobs, especially for young, inexperienced workers entering the workforce. It would also be devastating for single mothers struggling to support their children on minimum-wage earnings. Although minimum wage is not ideal for single parents, it at least provides an opportunity for them to develop skills that can lead to better-paying jobs. A minimum-wage hike will force small businesses to automate in many areas to save money, thus eliminating employment opportunities for single mothers.

Chantal Lovell, "Minimum-Wage Hike Is the Path to Poverty for Poor People," Nevada Policy Research Institute, October 29, 2014. NPRI.org. Copyright © 2014 Nevada Policy Research Institute. All rights reserved. Reproduced with permission.

As you read, consider the following questions:

1. According to Lovell, what percentage of people aged sixteen and older living beneath the poverty line do not work?

2. What percentage of those working at a minimum-wage job are single parents who work full-time?

3. How many minimum-wage workers receive a raise within a year of starting employment?

Apparently, Hillary Clinton is a little confused about the economy.

Last week [in October 2014] while speaking at a campaign rally in Massachusetts, she suggested raising the minimum wage wouldn't kill jobs, going on to say, "Don't let anybody tell you that it's corporations and businesses that create jobs."

Now, if a person fails to see that businesses are the job creators in the economy, it's understandable that such a person would also fail to see how raising the cost of doing business would kill jobs.

But just as Clinton's claim that businesses don't create jobs is ludicrous, so too is her belief that raising the minimum wage wouldn't be a devastating blow to jobs. Unfortunately, it's an all too common misunderstanding.

Last month, State Sen. Tick Segerblom announced plans to push a bill next year that would increase the minimum wage to $15 per hour in Nevada.

While it may sound appealing to double the pay of fast-food workers and other entry-level workers with one wave of the government's mandate wand, there's a big difference between good intentions and good results.

A Job Killer

What often gets lost in the emotional appeals of union-paid protesters supposedly representing minimum-wage workers is that the root cause of poverty isn't someone's wage, but whether or not that person works.

National statistics show that having a job is the best way to escape poverty. Of people ages 16 and older living beneath the poverty line, 67 percent do not work, while only 9 percent worked full-time and year-round. Conversely, over 81 percent of households within the top income bracket had at least two members working.

Given that not having a job and poverty are so closely correlated, raising the minimum wage—which even the nonpartisan Congressional Budget Office acknowledges would lead to substantial job losses—would have the exact opposite effect of what's intended. Instead of providing a higher wage to live on, the government would take away hundreds of thousands of individuals' ability to make a living. Young adults and those new to the workforce would be particularly harmed by such a move.

The Impact on Single Mothers

And what about single mothers working at minimum-wage jobs that the media so often tries to portray as the rule, rather than the exception? A lost job would hit them hardest of all.

If it's hard for a mom to feed her child while working at a minimum-wage job, it'll be even harder when she's unemployed. Fortunately such circumstances are rare. Only 4 percent of those making a minimum wage are single parents who work full-time. Instead, over half of those working for minimum wage are 24 years old or younger, and the majority of them—young and old workers alike—live in households that earn over 150 percent of the poverty line; many are still in school.

What's most encouraging is that those who take minimum-wage jobs typically earn raises quickly. Two-thirds of minimum-wage workers receive a raise within a year of starting employment.

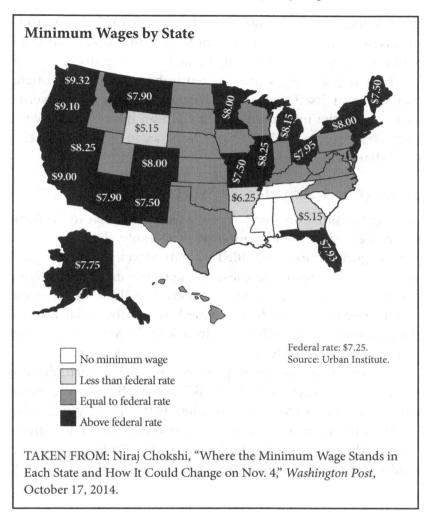

Minimum Wages by State

$9.32
$7.90
$5.15
$9.10
$8.00
$7.50
$8.15
$8.00
$8.25
$8.00
$8.25
$7.95
$9.00
$7.50
$7.90
$7.50
$6.25
$5.15
$7.75
$7.93

No minimum wage
Less than federal rate
Equal to federal rate
Above federal rate

Federal rate: $7.25.
Source: Urban Institute.

TAKEN FROM: Niraj Chokshi, "Where the Minimum Wage Stands in Each State and How It Could Change on Nov. 4," *Washington Post*, October 17, 2014.

To enjoy the higher salary that comes with job experience and improving your marketable skills, a worker has to be able to get a first job. But when the minimum wage is too high for inexperienced workers, the alternatives are heartbreaking.

Consider Las Vegas teen James "Bubba" Dukes. As a teen father struggling to graduate, he looked all over for a job—including at several fast-food establishments—but couldn't get so much as an interview. Because of the minimum wage—a government-imposed wage floor that harms unskilled and inexperienced laborers—Dukes couldn't find work. Unable to find a job legally, he eventually turned to selling drugs.

That tragic story, which currently happens far too often, would repeat itself even more frequently if Nevada government raised the minimum wage to $15 an hour as Segerblom proposes, or even to $10.10 per hour as suggested by President [Barack] Obama.

Supporting Inexperienced Workers

Making the situation worse for new workers is that technology has made it possible for employers to simply eliminate entire job categories previously filled by entry-level workers if government mandates make those workers too expensive to justify hiring. Many minimum-wage jobs, like those in fast-food establishments, are easily automated, so a substantial hike in the minimum wage will result in a Ronald McDonald robot taking your order instead of a smiling crew member.

Raising the minimum wage takes away the opportunity for inexperienced workers to learn skills and obtain the experience necessary to advance into other, better roles. While raising the minimum wage may sound noble, it cuts the bottom rung of the economic ladder for those, like Dukes, who most need—and want—to climb it.

Periodical and Internet Sources Bibliography

The following articles have been selected to supplement the diverse views presented in this chapter.

Shelley J. Correll	"Equal Pay? Not Yet for Mothers," Council on Contemporary Families, June 7, 2013.
Bryce Covert	"Working Single Mothers Are Disproportionately Likely to Be Poor," *ThinkProgress*, February 19, 2014.
Joanna Dreby	"Executive Action on Immigration Will Help Children and Families," Center for American Progress, March 3, 2015.
Mazie Hirono	"Immigration Reform and the Importance of Family," *The Hill*, December 31, 2014.
Olga Khazan	"How Welfare Reform Left Single Moms Behind," *Atlantic*, May 12, 2014.
Sara McLanahan and Christopher Jencks	"Was Moynihan Right?: What Happens to Children of Unmarried Mothers," *EducationNext*, vol. 15, no. 2, Spring 2015.
James T. Patterson	"Moynihan and the Single-Parent Family," *EducationNext*, vol. 15, no. 2, Spring 2015.
Delece Smith-Barrow	"Create a Plan for Success as a Single Parent in College," *U.S. News & World Report*, October 15, 2014.
Matthew Tinsley	"Parenting Alone: Work and Welfare in Single Parent Households," Policy Exchange, January 17, 2014.
Laura D'Andrea Tyson	"The Significance of the Minimum Wage for Women and Families," *Economix* (blog), *New York Times*, March 7, 2014.

For Further Discussion

Chapter 1

1. Kay Hymowitz argues that the nuclear family is more adaptable and more child-centered than the traditional extended family unit. Do you think the cultural shift from the extended family to the nuclear family after the Industrial Revolution benefitted families and society? Explain your reasoning.

2. In her viewpoint, Katie Roiphe points to a survey from the Pew Research Center showing that there is "a higher tolerance for gay couples raising children than there is for single mothers, with nearly seven in 10 Americans calling single motherhood a 'bad thing for society.'" What do you think of these findings? If you were included in this poll, what would be your response? Explain your reasoning.

3. Robert I. Lerman and W. Bradford Wilcox argue that two-parent families are more likely than one-parent families to experience economic stability. What reasons do Lerman and Wilcox give to support their argument? Do you agree? Why, or why not?

Chapter 2

1. Ellen Friedrichs argues that a double standard exists when it comes to single parenting, with single fathers looked upon as honorable and single mothers looked upon as irresponsible. Why do you think such a double standard exists? Do you think there is any basis for this double standard? Explain your reasoning.

2. Dave Taylor argues that being a single father is harder than being a single mother. He points out reasons why he thinks this to be true. How do you think Sash Milne would respond to Taylor? In your opinion, is it more dif-

ficult for a man or for a woman to be a single parent, or is the experience equally difficult for both? Explain.

3. In her viewpoint, Elizabeth Stuart points out that President Barack Obama, who was raised by a single mother, said, "In many ways, I came to understand the importance of fatherhood through its absence." What do you think President Obama meant by these words? Do you think a father plays a role in a child's life that a mother cannot fill? Explain.

Chapter 3

1. Barack Obama argues that it is necessary to provide full opportunities for women for the country's economic well-being. He mentions several policies that would help single mothers, including equal pay for equal work, paid family leave, subsidized day care, and raising the minimum wage. Of all the policies mentioned by Obama, which do you think would make the most positive impact on single-parent families? Explain your reasoning.

2. Marco Rubio argues that the link between marriage and economic security is undeniable and that the government should be doing more to promote marriage. He says that the tax code penalizes married couples and that a pro-family tax reform would end the marriage penalty. Do you think more couples would marry if such a tax break were in place for married couples? Explain.

3. Stephanie Mencimer discusses a federal program to promote marriage as a cure for poverty that spent hundreds of millions of taxpayer dollars and had no impact, or a negative impact, on the relationships of the couples who took part. What do you think the government's rationale is for spending money on such programs? Do you think such programs will have an effect on poverty reduction in America? Explain.

Chapter 4

1. Isabel V. Sawhill argues that an unwed birth, not divorce, is the most common way for a woman to enter into single parenthood. Therefore, she says that family planning is essential to strengthening families. Do you agree with Sawhill's argument? Why, or why not?

2. Mark W. Bennett discusses mandatory minimum sentences for drug offenders, saying that these sentences needlessly lock up nonviolent offenders and destroy families by fueling the cycle of poverty and addiction. He argues that sentencing reform would strengthen families. How do you think sentencing reform would help families? Cite text from the viewpoint to support your answer.

3. Thomas E. Perez argues that raising the minimum wage will result in greater economic security for families, while Chantal Lovell contends that an increased minimum wage would be harmful to working single parents. With which argument do you agree more, and why?

Organizations to Contact

The editors have compiled the following list of organizations concerned with the issues debated in this book. The descriptions are derived from materials provided by the organizations. All have publications or information available for interested readers. The list was compiled on the date of publication of the present volume; the information provided here may change. Be aware that many organizations take several weeks or longer to respond to inquiries, so allow as much time as possible.

Babble
website: www.babble.com

Babble is a network of blogs geared toward parents. Formerly known as iParenting Media, Babble provides news, articles, and personal essays about subjects such as parenting, pregnancy, entertainment, and child development. Babble features Babble Voices, a collection of top parent bloggers who provide information and their own ideas about parenting and child raising. Babble publishes a newsletter and features articles on single parenting, including "In the U.S. One in Four Kids Raised by Single Parent—Why Is That Number on the Rise?" and "Do Single Mothers Parent Better?"

Center on Children and Families
The Brookings Institution, 1775 Massachusetts Avenue NW
Washington, DC 20036
(202) 238-3158
website: www.brookings.edu/about/centers/ccf

The Center on Children and Families of the Brookings Institution studies policies that affect the well-being of American children, especially children in high-risk families, and their parents. The center focuses its resources on examining issues that have fueled domestic social policy debates in recent years; these include increasing economic mobility and opportunity for low-income families and reducing the growth of single-parent families. The center's website offers policy papers, reports, briefs, and blog posts, including "Families Are the Real Issue for Opportunity, Not Inequality" and "Celebrating Single Mothers by Choice."

Child Trends

7315 Wisconsin Avenue, Suite 1200W, Bethesda, MD   20814
(240) 223-9200 • fax: (240) 200-1238
website: www.childtrends.org

Child Trends is a nonprofit research center that provides valuable information and insights on the well-being of children and youth in the United States. It improves the lives and prospects of children by conducting high-quality research and sharing the results with practitioners and policy makers. Child Trends investigates family relationships that influence a child's development from birth through the transition to adulthood and examines all family and household structures, including children living with two parents, single parents, extended family members, foster parents, and adoptive parents. It publishes a weekly e-newsletter, and its website offers reports, news stories, videos, and the *Trend Lines* blog.

Council on Contemporary Families

305 East Twenty-Third Street, G1800, Austin, TX   78712
(512) 471-5514
website: https://contemporaryfamilies.org

The Council on Contemporary Families is a nonprofit, nonpartisan organization dedicated to providing the press and public with the latest research and best-practice findings about American families. Founded in 1996, the council's mission is to enhance the national understanding of how and why contemporary families are changing, what needs and challenges families face, and how these needs can best be met. The council's website offers opinion pieces, facts sheets, press releases, and reports such as "An Analysis of New Census Data on Family Structure, Education, and Income" and "Child-Rearing Norms and Practices in Contemporary American Families."

Extended Family
6303 Owensmouth Avenue, 10th Floor
Woodland Hills, CA   91367
(818) 937-3766
e-mail: info@extendedfamily.org
www.extendedfamily.org

Extended Family is a nonprofit charity designed to assist single parents and their families. It assists with clothes, food, housing, transportation, medical needs, education, and other expenses for single-parent families who are not financially well off and have little support from others. Its website offers media releases and news regarding the many single-parent families helped by the organization.

Family Research Council
801 G Street NW, Washington, DC   20001
(202) 393-2100 • fax: (202) 393-2134
website: www.frc.org

The Family Research Council (FRC) was founded in 1983 with the mission to champion marriage and family as the foundations of civilization. FRC shapes public debate and formulates public policy that upholds the institutions of marriage and the family. According to FRC, "families" are formed only by ties of blood, marriage, or adoption, and "marriage" is a union of one man and one woman. The council's website offers news, opinion pieces, policy papers, videos, radio broadcasts, and the *FRC Blog*, which features "What Is Marriage, and Why Does It Matter?" and "Society Cannot Escape Negative Outcomes of Marriage's Decline."

Focus on the Family
8605 Explorer Drive, Colorado Springs, CO   80920-1051
(800) 232-6459
website: www.focusonthefamily.com

Focus on the Family is a Christian organization that is dedicated to helping families thrive. It provides help and resources for couples to build healthy marriages that reflect God's design and for parents to raise their children according to morals and values grounded in biblical principles. The organization works to promote marriage as the foundation of family life and believes that children thrive best in a home where both mother and father are committed to raising them. The parenting section of Focus on the Family's website touches on the topic of single parenting with articles such as "Letting God Heal Broken Hearts" and the e-book *Help! I'm a Single Mom.*

Legal Momentum

5 Hanover Square, Suite 1502, New York, NY 10004
(212) 925-6635
website: www.legalmomentum.org

Founded in 1970, Legal Momentum works for a society in which all women and girls are economically secure, are empowered to make their own choices, and can live and work free of discrimination and violence. As the nation's oldest legal defense and education fund dedicated to advancing the rights of all women and girls, Legal Momentum works to advance these rights through litigation and public policy advocacy to secure economic and personal security for women. Its reports on single motherhood include "Single Motherhood in the United States—A Snapshot (2012)" and "Poverty Rates for Single Mothers Are Higher in the U.S. than in Other High Income Countries."

National Center for Fathering

10200 West Seventy-Fifth Street, #267
Shawnee Mission, KS 66204
e-mail: dads@fathers.com
website: www.fathers.com

The National Center for Fathering is a nonprofit research and education organization that seeks to provide fathers with the parenting skills they need to make them active participants in the lives of their children. The center offers innovative tools and resources to inspire and equip fathers to be more involved with their children, giving each child a better future and creating a family legacy that will impact future generations. The center's website provides testimonials, reports, news releases, and a blog, which features articles such as "Steady Through the Years: A Single Dad's Journey" and "Single Dads: It's a Small Club, Right?"

National Organization for Women (NOW)
1100 H Street NW, Suite 300, Washington, DC 20005
(202) 628-8669
website: www.now.org

The National Organization for Women (NOW) is the largest organization of feminist activists in the United States, with hundreds of thousands of contributing members and more than five hundred local and campus affiliates across the country. NOW is a multi-issue, multi-strategy organization that takes a holistic approach to women's rights and strives to bring about equality for all women. NOW advocates for a wide range of economic justice issues affecting women, including welfare reform, livable wages, job discrimination, pay equity, housing, and social security and pension reform. NOW has many publications available at its website, including "Labor Market Punishing to Mothers."

National Partnership for Women and Families
1875 Connecticut Avenue NW, Suite 650
Washington, DC 20009
(202) 986-2600 • fax: (202) 986-2539
e-mail: info@nationalpartnership.org
website: www.nationalpartnership.org

The National Partnership for Women and Families is a non-profit, nonpartisan organization that works for public policies that benefit women and families. For more than forty years, the group has been instrumental in promoting fairness for women in the workplace, fighting for women's reproductive health and rights, seeking access for women to affordable health care, and advancing policies that help women and men meet the dual demands of work and family. Its website offers news, press releases, fact sheets, congressional testimony, and a blog that features entries such as "Women, Work, and Family Health: A Balancing Act."

Parents Without Partners (PWP)
PO Box 215, Augusta, NJ   07822
(973) 702-0405
website: www.parentswithoutpartners.org

Parents Without Partners (PWP) is the largest nonprofit membership organization devoted to the welfare and interests of single parents and their children with thousands of members across the United States and Canada. It offers an environment for support, friendship, and the exchange of information that provides single parents and their children with opportunities to enhance personal growth and self-confidence. Its website offers links to resources such as articles, videos, books, and news stories related to single parenting.

Single Parent Advocate
e-mail: info@singleparentadvocate.org
website: www.singleparentadvocate.org

Single Parent Advocate is a nonprofit organization committed to educating and empowering single parents with resources, practical assistance, emotional encouragement, and social networking to better their lives and the lives of their children. Its website offers links to resources that provide strong and suitable aid for families as well as a blog that features posts such as "Getting Back into the Dating Game: A Guide for Single Parents," "Strengths of Single Parent Families," and "Successful Single Parenting."

Bibliography of Books

Janis Adams   *A Complete Guide for Single Moms: Everything You Need to Know About Raising Healthy, Happy Children on Your Own.* Ocala, FL: Atlantic Publishing Group, 2011.

Katrina Alcorn   *Maxed Out: American Moms on the Brink.* Berkeley, CA: Seal, 2013.

Elisabeth Badinter   *The Conflict: How Modern Motherhood Undermines the Status of Women.* New York: Metropolitan Books, 2010.

Sue Birdseye   *When Happily Ever After Shatters: Seeing God in the Midst of Divorce & Single Parenting.* Colorado Springs, CO: Focus on the Family, 2013.

Sandy Chalkoun   *Single Mother in Charge: How to Successfully Pursue Happiness.* Santa Barbara, CA: Praeger, 2010.

Andrew J. Cherlin   *The Marriage-Go-Round: The State of Marriage and the Family in America Today.* New York: Vintage, 2010.

Joanna Dreby   *Everyday Illegal: When Policies Undermine Immigrant Families.* Los Angeles: University of California Press, 2015.

Kathryn Edin and   *Promises I Can Keep: Why Poor Maria J. Kefalas   Women Put Motherhood Before Marriage.* Los Angeles: University of California Press, 2011.

Tony Evans	*Help and Hope for the Single Parent.* Chicago, IL: Moody Publishers, 2014.
Kathleen Gerson	*The Unfinished Revolution: Coming of Age in a New Era of Gender, Work, and Family.* New York: Oxford University Press, 2010.
Shante F. Green	*The Single Parent Survival Guide.* Bloomington, IN: WestBow Press, 2014.
Gretchen Gross and Patricia Livingston	*But Dad!: A Survival Guide for Single Fathers of Tween and Teen Daughters.* Lanham, MD: Rowman and Littlefield, 2012.
Arlie Hochschild and Anne Machung	*The Second Shift: Working Families and the Revolution at Home.* New York: Penguin Books, 2012.
Joy Jallah, Joseph Dowdy, Kathleen Klein, Santana Smith, and Shara Archuleta	*The Strength of Single Parenting.* Maugansville, MD: Joyfully Publishing Company, 2015.
Jorja Leap	*Project Fatherhood: A Story of Courage and Healing in One of America's Toughest Communities.* Boston, MA: Beacon Press, 2015.
Scott Lopez	*Single Parenting—Becoming the Best Parent for Your Child!* Seattle, WA: CreateSpace, 2010.
Donald Miller	*Father Fiction: Chapters for a Fatherless Generation.* New York: Howard Books, 2010.

Anne P. Mitchell   *They're Your Kids Too: The Single Father's Guide to Defending Your Fatherhood in a Broken Family Law System.* Henderson, NV: Isipp Publishing, 2011.

Anita Morawetz and Gillian Walker   *Brief Therapy with Single-Parent Families.* New York: Routledge, 2015.

Avital Norman Nathman   *The Good Mother Myth: Redefining Motherhood to Fit Reality.* Berkeley, CA: Seal Press, 2014.

Paul Raeburn   *Do Fathers Matter?: What Science Is Telling Us About the Parent We've Overlooked.* New York: Scientific American/Farrar, Straus and Giroux, 2014.

Norvin Richards   *The Ethics of Parenthood.* New York: Oxford University Press, 2010.

Lisa M. Rigas   *The Successful Single Mother: Proven Strategies for Creating an Incredible Lifestyle for You and Your Children.* Sarasota, FL: High Performance Marketing Solutions, 2013.

Sheryl Sandberg   *Lean In: Women, Work, and the Will to Lead.* New York: Knopf, 2013.

Natalia Sarkisian and Naomi Gerstel   *Nuclear Family Values, Extended Family Lives: The Power of Race, Class, and Gender.* New York: Routledge, 2012.

Rae Simons   *Single Parent Families.* Broomall, PA: Mason Crest, 2010.

John Sowers · · · · · · · *Fatherless Generation: Redeeming the Story.* Grand Rapids, MI: Zondervan, 2010.

Index

E

H

I

L

M

S